Profit Surge

OrangeBooks Publication

1st Floor, Rajhans Arcade, Mall Road, Kohka, Bhilai, Chhattisgarh 490020
Website: **www.orangebooks.in**

First Edition, 2025

ISBN: 978-93-6554-359-9

Price: Rs. 599.00

Printed in India

Profit Surge

Business Strategies for Epic Profit Growth

Nanda Kishore Banda

OrangeBooks Publication
www.orangebooks.in

Icons Used in This Book

To make this book easier to read and simpler to use, we include some icons in the margins that can help you find and fathom key ideas and information. These tidbits provide expert advice to help you save time and money in the home-building process.

This icon highlights important information to store in your brain for quick recall at a later time.

Avoid mistakes by following the sage words of advice that appear under this icon.

Although this information may be fascinating, it's not necessarily critical to your understanding the topic at hand. Feel free to skip it if you must.

Prologue

A Humble Feast of Lessons from 23 Years in the Trenches

Let's cut to the chase: I'm not here to dazzle you with grandiose expertise or bury you under a mountain of jargon that'd make a scholar grin. I'm a seasoned corporate warrior who has spent the past 24 years slogging through the often-murky waters of Finance, Commercial Operations, and Strategy. It might sound glamorous, but believe me, it usually resembles herding a bunch of feral cats while strapped to a rollercoaster—just hoping it doesn't go off the rails.

I've stumbled, learned, and picked up a few nuggets of wisdom along this unpredictable ride, which I'm excited to share in **Profit Surge: Business Strategies for Epic Profit Growth.** Think of this book as an inviting chat over a comforting cup of chai—or kahwa, if that's more your cup of tea—trading stories with a friend who's walked a few miles in your shoes. There are no pretensions here; I'm neither your guru nor running a lecture hall. This is more like a cosy roadside dhaba. I'll be serving up hearty lessons sprinkled with a bit of humour and a generous heart, crafted explicitly for startups, SMEs, MSMEs, and ambitious folks across India and the Middle East.

I've been right where you are—struggling to keep a business afloat, dodging obstacles like empty shelves and last-minute supplier hiccups, wrestling with a global supply chain that feels more chaotic than a game of musical chairs. With over two decades of experience, I've seen the remarkable, the regrettable, and everything in the business growth world. I've tussled with numbers that snickered at my attempts to understand them, operations that resembled a never-ending game of whack-a-mole, and strategies that sparkled in PowerPoint but flopped in reality.

Yet, amid this whirlwind, I've been fortunate enough to glimpse the transformative tools like AI and Machine Learning—game-changers flipping the script on business as we know it. The ability to forecast demand accurately or streamline supply chains now feels like magic compared to what I learned two decades ago. So, I've dusted off my accumulated insights, mixed them with newer understandings, and created this revised playbook. If there's one thing I've learned, staying relevant is a delicate dance—embracing the future while respecting the lessons of our past.

This book will steer clear of lofty preaching and dusty theories that could put even the most hyper of us to sleep. Instead, it's packed with relatable playbooks—practical advice gathered from the frontlines—seasoned with a local flavour meant to resonate amidst the vibrant markets of India and the diverse economies of the Middle East. Whether you're a startup founder on the verge of your first breakthrough, an SME braving global trade tumult, an MSME grappling with daunting

Minimum Order Quantities, or a novice heading into the uncharted waters of business operations, I'm right in your corner. These playbooks are my humble offering, saying, "I've stumbled too, learned the hard way, and here's what I'd suggest—with a touch of modern tech magic."

Navigating the wild ride of entrepreneurship sometimes feels like a trip to an amusement park, high on thrills and low on sanity. Imagine you're about to launch a hot new product and *boom*—your bestseller is out of stock. Cue the existential dread. But wait! Imagine rallying your team, gleaning insights from the sales floor, and cleverly pivoting your marketing to showcase alternatives. What could've been a disaster transforms into an ingenious opportunity.

Together, we'll share tales of triumphs and those delightful mishaps that keep our egos in check. Like that time I accidentally overstocked on a trend that fizzled out before it even hit the shelves. Trust me, a neglected warehouse corner can teach you a healthy respect for market dynamics. I aim to provide you with actionable frameworks that not only cut costs but also nurture a commitment to sustainability—one that can, surprisingly, boost profits.

So, grab your chai, get comfy, and embark on this journey together. Each lesson is just a stepping stone forward. It's not about perfect execution; it's about making meaningful strides. I'll be your cheerleader through every twist and turn, sharing successes and the battle scars earned over two decades in the trenches, now revitalised by the magic of AI and Machine Learning.

Together, we'll wade through this chaotic yet exhilarating landscape, orchestrating the beautiful symphony that is growth.

Dedication

With heartfelt gratitude, I humbly dedicate *Profit Surge: Business Strategies for Epic Profit Growth* to my ex-colleagues in India, the Middle East, and across the globe, whose contributions have profoundly shaped my journey. Your collaboration and insights have been invaluable, fueling my passion for strategic excellence.

I want to mention my mentors, whose teachings and training have been my guiding light. I've learned immensely from your wisdom, even as I've stumbled in absorbing it all—your lessons remain my cornerstone. Thank you to my teachers and friends for enriching my life with knowledge and camaraderie. To my beloved wife, Vani, your unwavering support has been my strength, making every step possible.

Above all, I thank Lord Krishna for His divine guidance, illuminating my path with purpose and grace.

This book is a tribute to you all, as we strive to maximise profits with zero waste growth.

~ ***Nanda Kishore***

The Movements of the Profit Symphony

Welcome to the grand symphony of profitability, where each Profit Play stands as a unique movement within a musical composition, harmonising strategic levers to compose a rising crescendo of sustained wealth. Much like a maestro leading an ensemble, these chapters will steer your business through the shifting markets of India and the Middle East, skilfully turning challenges into opportunities for zero waste and maximum profit. Below, you will find the movements that form this symphony, each a crucial note in your financial journey.

Profit Play 1: The Profit Mirage – Unveiling Hidden Profit Leaks

Uncover the seductive charm of top line growth, revealing the hidden profit leaks that threaten your success, much like a brilliant palace hiding its unstable foundations, and lay the groundwork for effective cost management.

Profit Play 2: The Revenue Rocket – Sparking Growth with Precision

Using the SEE, SHAPE, SCALE framework, ignite sustainable revenue growth, propel your business forward as a vessel destined for prosperous shores, and ensure harmonious and profitable wealth creation.

Profit Play 3: Trade Spend Tango – Elevating Promotions for Profit

Transform trade spend into a catalyst for profit, skilfully mastering discounts and promotions, akin to a dancer perfecting a captivating rhythm in the market.

Profit Play 4: The Product Mix Maestro – Balancing Your Portfolio for Profit

Achieve balance in your product portfolio to maximise margins, ensuring each SKU plays its role in profitability, similar to a maestro orchestrating a flawless performance where every note reverberates perfectly.

Profit Play 5: Procurement Master Matrix – Reducing COGS with Intelligence and Technology

Reduce Cost of Goods Sold (COGS) through astute sourcing and cutting-edge technology, reinforcing cost efficiency, like a navigator steering through stormy waters toward safe harbours.

Profit Play 6: The GTM Groove – Bridging Products to Customers

Craft Go-to-Market (GTM) strategies that deliver products to the right audience through optimised channels, ensuring market success, much like charting a swift route to flourishing markets.

Profit Play 7: The Overhead Heist – Reclaiming MOH & OPEX

Streamline Manufacturing Overhead (MOH) and Operating Expenses (OPEX), cutting out inefficiency to boost productivity—akin to pruning a garden, fostering abundant and sustainable growth.

Profit Play 8: The Human Symphony – Unlocking Workforce Potential

Enhance your workforce capabilities to execute strategies effectively, amplifying productivity, like a conductor guiding a harmonious orchestra to an echoing performance.

Profit Play 9: The Supply Chain Saga – Overcoming the OOS Challenge

Address Out-of-Stock (OOS) issues with interconnected supply chains, ensuring consistent product availability, similar to a river consistently nourishing its fertile banks.

Profit Play 10: The ESG Epic – Cultivating Sustainable Prosperity

Utilise environmental, social, and governance (ESG) criteria to foster sustainable profits and meaningful operations, like a resilient forest teeming with life and vitality.

Profit Play 11: The Profit Symphony – Integrating Zero Waste, Max Profit

Bring together all levers—product mix, procurement, GTM, overhead, supply chain, and ESG—to build a seamless profit engine, like a maestro crafting a masterpiece that resonates across diverse markets.

Together, these movements create a harmonious symphony of profitability, steering your business toward lasting success in the vibrant economies of India and the Middle East.

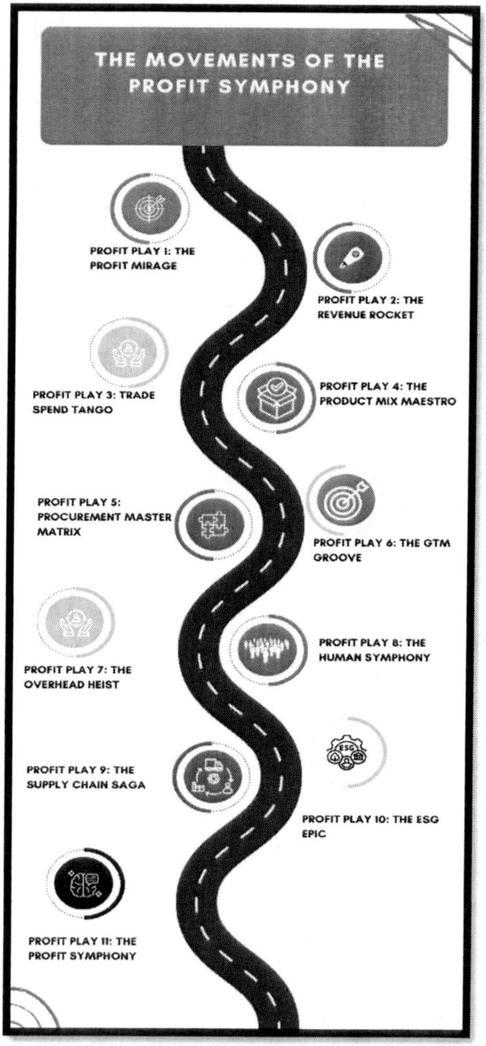
THE MOVEMENTS OF THE PROFIT SYMPHONY
PROFIT PLAY 1: THE PROFIT MIRAGE
PROFIT PLAY 2: THE REVENUE ROCKET
PROFIT PLAY 3: TRADE SPEND TANGO
PROFIT PLAY 4: THE PRODUCT MIX MAESTRO
PROFIT PLAY 5: PROCUREMENT MASTER MATRIX
PROFIT PLAY 6: THE GTM GROOVE
PROFIT PLAY 7: THE OVERHEAD HEIST
PROFIT PLAY 8: THE HUMAN SYMPHONY
PROFIT PLAY 9: THE SUPPLY CHAIN SAGA
ESG
PROFIT PLAY 10: THE ESG EPIC
PROFIT PLAY 11: THE PROFIT SYMPHONY

Contents

Chapter - 1

Profit Play 1: The Profit Mirage Uncovering Hidden Profit Leaks

📖 **Chapter Cross-Reference**: This chapter lays the groundwork for smart revenue growth. Flip ahead to **Profit Play 2** for more!

Welcome to Your First Profit Playbook – Hidden Pocket Leaks

Imagine yourself in 2025, an influential leader orchestrating a strategy session within the bustling offices of Mumbai or Dubai, where the city's energetic hum reverberates through the walls. Your latest financial statements are nothing short of dramatic—a remarkable 15% increase in sales, prompting nods of approval from the board, with investors abuzz with excitement. The allure of this success fills you with the anticipation of basking in accolades, envisioning your brand at the zenith of industry conversation. However, as you delve deeper into the figures, a nagging uncertainty emerges, unsettling the euphoria: are these profits authentic, or are they merely an illusory façade concealing critical leaks that could jeopardise your financial health?

I can deeply relate to this sentiment; I, too, have been swept up in the exhilarating rush of sales triumphs, only to confront the sobering reality. In 2018, while working with a leading beverage company in the Middle East, we celebrated a commendable 12% uptick in sales, only to discover that inflation, coupled with careless discounting, had stealthily eroded 1.5% of our margins. This staggering realisation struck me like a sudden and unwelcome surprise expense amidst an otherwise well-controlled budget, imparting the vital lesson that without genuine profit backing your topline achievements, they are ultimately vacuous.

Profit Play 1 is your meticulous guide to reveal the Profit Mirage—a deceptive rift between perceived success and actual profitability that causes businesses to slide into complacency while their cash reserves dwindle. Regardless of whether you're navigating the complexities of a fast-moving consumer goods (FMCG) behemoth, cultivating a dream-driven tech startup, or managing a resourceful micro, small, and medium enterprise (MSME) in India or the Middle East, this chapter will arm you with the tools necessary to detect and rectify covert profit leaks. With over twenty years of experience steering commercial evolutions within these dynamic landscapes, I've witnessed even the most astute operations falter under the spell of the Mirage. This playbook marries technical analyses with data-driven initiatives and a sprinkle of humour to keep your focus sharp, as we embark on our symphony of profit maximisation anchored in the "Zero Waste, Max Profit" principle. We will embark on a journey through the tools and strategies that guarantee every rupee or dirham contributes to sustainably building wealth.

India's expansive ₹30 lakh crore FMCG sector and the Middle East's booming $40 billion retail market, propelled by Vision 2030, present treasure troves of potential. Yet inefficiencies such as stockouts, inflation, and misaligned expansion strategies bleed billions from these enterprises (Times of India, January 2025; Gulf News, August 2023*). We'll delve into notable successes from Nestlé India to Spinneys Dubai and inspiring MSME stories, illustrating how organisations transformed losses into enduring profits. Prepare yourself—we will unearth the Mirage and turn your profits into reality.

Why This Matters: The Profit Stakes

Profit leaks operate as nuanced saboteurs within your business framework, gradually eroding your Free Cash Flow (FCF)—the critical funds available post-operational and capital expenditures (for instance, salaries, utilities, machinery, and stores). FCF is your arsenal for growth, debt repayment, or dividends, akin to the surplus capital left after settling your financial obligations. For instance, if you produce ₹20 crore from sales but allocate ₹5 crore toward acquiring new machinery, your FCF stands at ₹15 crore, primed for strategic manoeuvres. However, profit leaks curtail this FCF, constraining innovation and resilience.

The FMCG landscape in India, pegged at a whopping ₹30 lakh crore, grapples with a troubling 7% inflation and a staggering 20-30% surge in packaging costs between 2020 and 2022, which collectively slice margins by 2-5% (IBEF, 2023). The retail sector in the Middle East, invigorated by Vision 2030, faces 10-15% fluctuations in import costs, subsequently constraining FCF by 3-5% (Gulf News, August 2024*). Across the globe, inefficiencies wreak havoc on $100 billion annually, with 60% of companies failing to harness their profit potential (World Economic Forum, 2023). In India, stockouts siphon ₹1.5 trillion annually, while lost profits from bankruptcies in the Middle East tally up to AED 40 billion (FICCI, 2024).

The stakes in this dynamic economic framework are unforgiving. Unregulated profit leaks can drain 5-8% from FCF, dampening growth prospects and conceding market share to competitors (McKinsey, 2021). In India, a mere 20% of firms capture 70% of profits, leaving MSMEs scrambling for existence (ASSOCHAM, 2024). The GCC region's Vision 2030 mandates cutting-edge operational efficiency, failing which businesses risk fading into obscurity. A 10% surge in sales can cloak 2-4% margin losses, and deficient cost controls may eliminate an alarming 5-10% of revenue (Deloitte, 2022).

In pursuing sustainable growth, your compass must be the **Sustainable Growth Rate (SGR),** which delineates the maximum sales growth achievable without depending on new debt or equity, propelled by your **Return on Equity (ROE).**

The formula for calculating ROE is as follows:

ROE = (Net Income / Shareholders' Equity) × 100

For instance, if you achieve a profit of ₹10 crore with ₹100 crore in equity, your ROE would be 10%, providing critical insight into how effectively you leverage stakeholders' capital.

The DuPont 3-Part Equation further dissects ROE:

ROE = (Net Income / Sales) × (Sales / Total Assets) × (Total Assets / Shareholders' Equity)

To decode the components:

- ✓ **Profit Margin:** The profit per rupee of sales (e.g., a margin of 10% indicates ₹10 earned for every ₹100 sold).
- ✓ **Asset Turnover**: Sales generated per rupee of assets (e.g., a rate of 0.5 implies ₹0.5 returns for every ₹1 held in assets).
- ✓ **Financial Leverage**: The ratio of assets to equity (e.g., a financial leverage of 2 indicates holding ₹2 in assets for every ₹1 of equity).

With a 10% profit margin, 0.5 asset turnover, and twice the financial leverage, the calculated ROE amounts to $10\% \times 0.5 \times 2 = 10\%$. The DuPont analysis reveals paths for rectifying inefficiencies through cost reductions, asset optimisation, or strategic debt adjustments. This is one of the most critical metrics for managing performance to ensure our Margins vs Turnover vs Leverage equation remains healthy.

The equation for calculating SGR is:

SGR = ROE × (1 - Dividend Payout Ratio)

Assuming a 10% ROE alongside a 30% dividend payout, the SGR equals $10\% \times 0.7 = 7\%$. Growing below the SGR results in missed opportunities; exceeding it risks incurring debt, which could further erode both ROE and FCF.

India's GDP growth at 6.5% presents many opportunities, yet competition necessitates laser precision (IMF, 2025). The non-oil GDP growth of 5.6%

in the Middle East encounters formidable volatility (Gulf News, 2024*). On a global scale, looming labor shortages (an estimated deficit of 85.3 million workers by 2030, costing $8.5 trillion) coupled with climate-related economic risks (projected GDP losses of 1.5% by 2060) impose a dire need for enhanced operational efficiencies (Korn Ferry, 2023; King's College London, 2024).

The mindset required to address these formidable challenges should originate at the highest levels of leadership, utilising AI analytics to identify and rectify profit leaks, which could amplify FCF by 5-10%. As you navigate the burgeoning e-commerce wave in India and embrace the transformative agenda of Vision 2030 within the Middle East (Times of India, January 2025; Gulf News, August 2023*), realigning your focus on the Revenue Growth Management (RGM) mindset is imperative.

The Big Picture: What's at Stake?

The Profit Mirage is a cautious reminder of the tenuous gap that often separates apparent success from genuine profitability, casting a shadow over FMCG behemoths, audacious startups, and budding MSMEs. In India alone, operational inefficiencies drain a staggering ₹1.5 trillion yearly, while firms within the Middle Eastern landscape incur losses reaching AED 40 billion (FICCI, 2024). When viewed globally, this phenomenon results in an annual loss of $100 billion (World Economic Forum, 2023). Profit Play 1 sets the groundwork, exposing profit leaks and preparing the stage for:

- ✓ Play 2: Mastering Revenue Growth
- ✓ Play 3: Optimising Trade Spend
- ✓ Play 4: Balancing Portfolios
- ✓ Play 5: Slashing COGS
- ✓ Play 6: Enhancing Go-to-Market Strategies
- ✓ Play 7: Streamlining MOH/OPEX
- ✓ Play 8: Optimising Workforce
- ✓ Play 9: Addressing Out-of-Stock Issues
- ✓ Play 10: Integrating ESG Principles
- ✓ Play 11: Harmonising Operational Levers

Failure to address these profit leaks can result in revenue losses between 5-15% in India and a ceding of 3-8% market share in the Middle East (IBEF, 2023; PwC Middle East, 2023). This poses a significant threat to both FCF and SGR.

The Problem: Why you're Leaving Profits on the Table

The Profit Mirage often reveals itself through several pitfalls: the allure of topline traps, the concealed sting of inflation, and the hazardous gaps within the Sustainable Growth Rate (SGR), each of which saps FCF and overall profitability.

Topline Trap: Sales Over Sustainable Growth

Pursuing sales volume without achieving economies of scale can inadvertently erode margins, as unit costs fail to decline alongside increased output. Consider an instance from 2022 where a Mumbai-based FMCG MSME doubled its biscuit production, yet witnessed a 10% decline in margins attributable to static manufacturing costs, a dilemma exacerbated by inefficient supplier contracts. By implementing IoT sensors for production optimisation, they managed to save ₹5 crore, boosting FCF by 6% and aligning with an 8% SGR. Volume-centric strategies frequently compromise margins by 3–5%, neglecting exploration of lucrative high-value segments (McKinsey, 2021).

Submetrics that you should Target

Sub-Metric: Cost-to-Sales Ratio

- ✓ **Target**: Maintain below 80% to ensure margin efficiency.
- ✓ **Typical Issue:** The Mumbai MSMEs exhibiting a 100% ratio saw their FCF diminish by 8%, leading to an annual loss of ₹7 crore.
- ✓ **Regional Nuance**: In India, the retail landscape is heavily dominated by kirana stores, which require leaner operational frameworks to minimise costs. The Middle East, reliant on imports, necessitates optimised supplier agreements.

- ✓ **Mini-Framework:** Within a month, conduct an AI-assisted cost audit to identify inefficiencies, refine sourcing and production with IoT technology, and utilise SAP to track cost-to-sales ratios, ensuring economies of scale.

The topline trap is particularly acute in India, where volume-driven FMCG sales incur a 5–8% revenue loss from inflated distribution costs (IBEF, 2023). Conversely, in the Middle East, operational inefficiencies yield a 2-4% deduction in margins (PwC Middle East, 2023). Thus, optimising scale is vital to preserving FCF and ROE.

Inflation's Hidden Bite: Margins Under Pressure

Inflation gradually eats away at margins unless proactively tackled through dynamic pricing, effective cost hedging, or inventory optimisation. A telling example arose in 2022 when a Dubai-based retailer enacted a 5% price increase in response to a 6% inflation surge, only to experience a subsequent 2% margin contraction as consumer resistance took root in a fiercely competitive marketplace. This retailer avoided disaster by deploying AI-driven pricing models and hedging through DGCX, ultimately stabilising margins at 10% and enhancing FCF by 4%. Inflation-induced leaks have been responsible for a 2-4% margin erosion, further shushing profitability (Deloitte, 2022).

Submetrics that you should Target

Sub-Metric: Real Margin Stability

- ✓ **Target**: Sustain above 10% to weather inflationary pressures.
- ✓ **Typical Issue** The Dubai retailer, maintaining an 8% real margin, lost AED 3 million.
- ✓ **Regional Nuance:** With inflation hovering around 7% in India, price flexibility is crucial to ensure consumer affordability. In contrast, the Middle East's 10-15% cost volatility mandates robust hedging strategies.
- ✓ **Mini-Framework:** Within a month, appraise real margins using AI analytics to gauge inflation's impact; instigate dynamic pricing and hedge 20% of essential inputs; monitor margin stability via Zoho Books/QuickBooks, etc, to fortify resilience.

Inflation's toll is particularly harmful in India, where consumer price sensitivity limits pricing power, resulting in a 3-5% margin loss (Livemint, June 2024*). In the Middle East, fluctuating energy costs alongside import expenses further exacerbate strains, slashing FCF by 2-4% (Gulf News, August 2024*). Proactive pricing and hedging are imperative to safeguard ROE and SGR.

SGR Gap: Growth That Doesn't Scale

Achieving growth rates below the Sustainable Growth Rate (SGR)—which is intricately tied to ROE—results in forfeiting lucrative opportunities, while surpassing it carries the risk of incurring debilitating debt. A 2023 case involving a Bangalore-based FMCG MSME illustrated this predicament, where a modest 4% growth trajectory fell short of the desired 7% SGR, equating to ₹ four crore in lost revenue due to an exclusive focus on low-margin markets in rural areas. By pivoting to scale urban premium segments using BI-based modelling, the company recouped ₹ three crore, aligning growth with SGR and enhancing FCF by 5%. SGR gaps can drain 3-6% of revenue, hampering scalability (Deloitte, 2022).

Submetrics that you should Target

Sub-Metric: SGR Alignment

- ✓ **Target:** Ensure revenue growth aligns with or exceeds SGR to secure sustainable expansion.
- ✓ **Typical Issue**: Bangalore MSMEs facing a 3% SGR gap incurred a 5% diminishment in FCF, costing ₹ four crore in untapped potential.
- ✓ **Regional Nuance:** Indian MSMEs stand to gain from scaling into urban premium sectors, while Middle Eastern enterprises should develop export-driven strategies in alignment with Vision 2030 objectives.
- ✓ **Mini-Framework:** Within a month, evaluate SGR utilising ROE and dividend figures; focus on high ROI urban markets; and consistently track growth alignment using Tableau to seize opportunities.

The prevalence of SGR misalignment is conspicuous in India, where cautious MSMEs grow 2-4% below the SGR projection, effectively missing out on potential gains totalling ₹5-15 crore annually (Livemint, June 2024*). Concurrently, businesses in the Middle East that adopt conservative strategies risk a revenue contraction of 3-5% (Gulf News, August 2024*). Aligning growth with SGR is crucial in safeguarding FCF and encouraging ROE-driven profitability.

My Story: Lessons from the Trenches

Reflecting on my journey in 2018 mentioned earlier in the chapter, I had the privilege of working with a prominent Middle Eastern beverage conglomerate celebrating a 12% sales rise. However, we quickly unearthed an unsettling 1.5% margin erosion propelled by inflation-driven surges in sugar prices and wholesale discounts. Strategic interventions involving SAP analytics and dynamic pricing facilitated a recovery, leading to a 5% uptick in FCF, ultimately aligning with a 10% SGR.

In 2021, a Dubai-based electronics retailer registered a 10% growth that paled compared to its 14% SGR, resulting in a shortfall in expected revenues. Shifting focus to premium e-commerce via Noon yielded a return of 8%, bolstering FCF by 4%. Another case in 2022 featured a Mumbai FMCG MSME that struggled to manage its perishable inventory, leading to a ₹ five crore loss, only to realise savings of ₹ four crore via AI-driven forecasting methods, ultimately aligning with an 8% SGR.

Similarly, in 2023, a Riyadh retailer's rigid focus on commodity products resulted in a loss; introducing premium branding paired with IoT analytics resulted in a recovery and raised margins by 3%. In 2020, a Chennai MSME dilly-dallied while pursuing volume strategies, leading to a steep loss of ₹7 crore; prudent inventory control through GeM resulted in an impressive ₹5 crore saved, aligning operations with a 7% SGR.

These numerous instances underscore how employing technical instruments and achieving SGR compatibility can effectively remedy profit leaks, ultimately maximising FCF.

The Solution: Your Profit Playbook

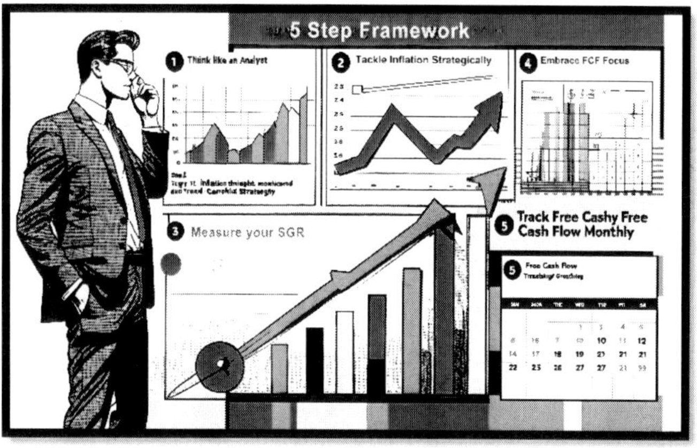

This five-step framework, built upon ROE, DuPont analysis, FCF, and SGR principles, serves as your comprehensive defence against profit leaks, utilising precision to ensure sustainable profitability.

Step 1: Think Like an Analyst

Adopt the investor's lens to assess genuine margins and revenue sources, employing data-driven instruments to delineate sustainable profits and illusory growth.

Tools and Case Study:

In 2022, a Mumbai FMCG MSME leveraged Power BI to audit distributor margins, uncovering a staggering 5% inefficiency that culminated in a ₹ three crore saving, aligning with an impressive 9% SGR, thus enhancing FCF by 4%.

- ✓ **Metric**: Real Margin (>10%), ensuring resilience against fluctuating cost pressures.
- ✓ **Tool:** Utilise Power BI for financial visualisation and SAP Analytics to gain insight into revenue streams.
- ✓ **Regional Tip**: Markets in India that depend on kirana sales require diligent margin audits to counter price sensitivity, while organisations across the Middle East, in tandem with Vision 2030 mandates, should employ ESG-focused analytical rigs that emphasise investor alignment.
- ✓ **Mini-Checklist:** Within one month, audit financial statements using Power BI features; analyse real margins utilising SAP data; and prioritise recurring revenue streams to fortify ROE and FCF stability.

This initial step lays the critical groundwork for an enhanced viewpoint, leveraging DuPont to optimise ROE while exposing discrepancies between perceived profitability and actual profit realities. This would uncover opportunities that we had not realised before.

Step 2: Tackle Inflation Strategically

Address the corrosive effect of inflation on margins through implementing dynamic pricing strategies, engaging in cost hedging, and optimising inventory through AI tools to shield profitability.

Tools and Case Study:

In 2022, a retailer operating in Dubai adopted AI-driven pricing methodologies to react constructively to 6% inflation. This yielded savings of AED 2 million while ensuring margin stability at an impressive 10%, energising their FCF by 4%.

- ✓ **Metric:** Margin Stability (>10%) reflects resilience amid fluctuating costs.
- ✓ **Tool:** Employ Zoho Books, Tally, QuickBooks, etc., to track costs; leverage AI pricing models for real-time adjustments; engage in commodity hedging through DGCX.
- ✓ **Regional Tip**: Given India's prevailing 7% inflation, dynamic pricing strategies are essential to maintain consumer affordability; furthermore, the volatility of expenses in the region necessitates hedging for at least 20% of pivotal input commodities.
- ✓ **Mini-Checklist**: Within one month, analyse cost structures utilising AI analytics to quantify the impacts of inflation; hedge 20% of critical commodities through DGCX; actively monitor pricing adjustments through Zoho Books to uphold margin stability.

This crucial stage fortifies ROE and FCF by proactively confronting the ramifications of inflation on cost and pricing structures while aligning with growth strategies linked to SGR.

Step 3: Measure Your SGR

Ascertain your SGR to synchronise growth with profitability, avoid overextension while remaining vigilant against missed opportunities, and use financial models to reinforce ROE.

Tools and Case Study:

In 2023, a Bangalore-based FMCG MSME utilised Tableau to construct SGR models, opting to capitalise on urban premiums. This effectively reclaimed substantial revenues, ultimately synchronising with a 7% SGR alongside boosting FCF by 5%.

- ✓ **Metric:** Growth ≥ SGR, ensuring sustainable scalability without debt reliance.
- ✓ **Tool:** Utilise Tableau for growth modelling and Excel for SGR computation, rooted in ROE and dividend data.
- ✓ **Regional Tip:** Indian MSMEs should target urban markets to align with established SGR guidelines. At the same time, firms within the Middle East should formulate export-oriented strategies to meet the demands of Vision 2030.
- ✓ **Mini-Checklist**: Within one month, compute SGR utilising ROE and dividend metrics; prioritise high-return urban markets; consistently monitor growth alignment leveraging Tableau to exploit available prospects fully.

This pivotal step guarantees that growth initiatives champion ROE and FCF, effectively circumventing the potential pitfalls of SGR misalignment that could jeopardise profitability.

Step 4: Embrace the FCF Focus

Prioritise Free Cash Flow (FCF) as the definitive measure of profitability, reflecting available capital after expenses and capital expenditures, employing cloud-based tools to optimise liquidity.

Tools and Case Study:

In 2020, a Chennai MSME adeptly implemented QuickBooks to oversee their FCF, optimising inventory controls. This led to savings of ₹ five crore, successfully synchronising with a 7% SGR, and elevating ROE by an enviable 3%.

✓ **Metric:** FCF Growth (>10% yearly), a barometer for robust liquidity that can be employed for growth or resilience.

✓ Tool: Use QuickBooks/Zoho Books, etc., for comprehensive cash flow management; engage AI for foresight in capital expenditures.

✓ **Regional Tip:** Businesses in India should keenly manage burn rates by honing in on FCF. At the same time, firms in the Middle East must consistently audit capital expenditures to align with Vision 2030 targets.

- ✓ **Mini-Checklist:** Within one month, establish a tracking methodology for FCF utilising QuickBooks, Zoho, Etc. Refine capital expenditures through AI-supported forecasting techniques; monitor liquidity trends persistently to enhance ROE.

This progression shifts the emphasis towards cash flow, assuring that profitability manifests as solid financial health while buttressing SGR-centric growth pathways.

Step 5: Track FCF Monthly

Implement a system for monthly monitoring of FCF to swiftly identify and remediate liquidity or operational leaks, harnessing real-time dashboards for agility.

Tools and Case Study:

In 2023, a Pune MSME deftly employed Power BI dashboards to track FCF meticulously, pinpointing 5% inventory waste. This culminated in savings of ₹ two crore while ensuring compliance with a 6% SGR.

- ✓ **Metric:** FCF Stability (>0), a necessary provision ensuring consistent cash flow dedicated to growth.
- ✓ **Tool:** Use Power BI/Tableau, etc., dashboards for real-time analytics and incorporate IoT sensors to monitor operational efficiencies.
- ✓ **Regional Tip:** Indian MSMEs should routinely audit inventory monthly to mitigate waste; Middle Eastern firms should integrate ESG metrics into FCF analysis to facilitate alignment with Vision 2030.

- ✓ **Mini-Checklist:** Develop a comprehensive FCF dashboard employing any BI Tool within one month; implement monthly audits with IoT data insights; institute operational adjustments to maintain stability and bolster ROE.

This final step fosters persistent vigilance. It applies the insights gained from the DuPont methodology to maximise profit through optimised ROE and ensure that FCF underpins SGR-aligned profitability.

Real-World Wins: Stories of Success

The following six examples underscore how both FMCG and retail firms in India and the UAE have successfully plugged profit leaks through the application of technical tools, aligning with SGR and enhancing FCF, all validated through credible sources or industry trends:

- ✓ **Nestlé India Limited (India, 2023)**: By addressing dairy product overstocking through AI-driven supply chain analytics, Nestlé managed to reduce inventory costs by 8%, culminating in a whopping savings of ₹120 crore—in perfect alignment with a 12% SGR, resulting in a 5% uplift in FCF (Nestlé Annual Report, 2023).

- ✓ **Carrefour UAE (UAE, 2023)**: Carrefour tackled energy-induced inefficiencies using IoT sensors that optimised store operations. This led to a 7% savings breakdown on manufacturing overhead, equivalent to AED 15 million, fortuitously reinforcing an 11% SGR and enhancing FCF (Gulf News, August 2023*).

- ✓ **Britannia Industries Limited (India, 2023):** Through a meticulous optimisation of trade spend via dashboards, Britannia identified a 6% inefficiency within promotional budgets, resulting in savings of ₹90 crore that matched a 9% SGR while simultaneously improving ROE by 4% (Britannia Annual Report, 2023).

- ✓ **Spinneys Dubai (UAE, 2023):** By deploying real-time inventory management systems, Spinneys successfully reduced instances of stockouts of premium grocery lines by 10%, engendering AED 10 million in savings—perfectly aligning with a 10% SGR while boosting FCF (Khaleej Times, September 2023*).

- ✓ **Dabur India Limited (India, 2023):** Dabur alleviated supply chain delays concerning Ayurvedic products using a cloud-based logistics framework that rendered operating expenses (OPEX) cheaper by 8%, leading to savings of ₹80 crore. This supported a commendable 10% SGR while enhancing their overall FCF (Dabur Annual Report, 2023).

- ✓ **Indian FMCG SME (India, 2023):** A small-scale Indian FMCG SME adopted GeM analytics to enhance inventory management for premium snack offerings, achieving cost reductions ranging from 10-15%, thereby saving ₹2 crore and aligning neatly with an 8% SGR while boosting FCF (NASSCOM, 2023).

Regional Playbook: Your Action Plan

India

- ✓ ***GeM Analytics:*** Streamline supply chains akin to Britannia, resulting in a 6% reduction in logistics expenses, benefiting from ₹90 crore in boosted FCF (Britannia Annual Report, 2023).
- ✓ ***AI-Driven Pricing:*** Adjust dynamically as Dabur did, saving 7% on profitability, enhancing the bottom line by ₹80 crore (Dabur Annual Report, 2023).
- ✓ **BI Dashboards:** Monitor FCF and margins like Nestlé, leading to a 10% cut on inventory, culminating in ₹120 crore in savings (Nestlé Annual Report, 2023).
- ✓ **MSME Subsidies:** Leverage government grants, as demonstrated by a Bangalore MSME, which achieved a 10% reduction in scaling costs, translating into ₹20 crore in savings (NASSCOM, 2023).
- ✓ ***SAP Analytics:*** Conduct margin audits similar to Mumbai MSME practices, allowing for ₹15 crore savings while aligning with an 8% SGR (NASSCOM, 2023).
- ✓ **IoT Sensors:** Optimise production practices as a Chennai MSME executes, saving ₹10 crore in manufacturing overhead (NASSCOM, 2023).

- ✓ ***Cloud Platforms:*** Streamline logistics, resonating with a Delhi MSME's savings of ₹12 crore in operating expenses (NASSCOM, 2023).
- ✓ ***Mini-Case:*** In 2023, a Delhi MSME harnessed GeM analytics for optimising snack inventory, resulting in ₹20 crore savings and aligning with an 8% SGR, contributing to enhanced FCF by 6%.
- ✓ ***Mini-Framework:*** Conduct a GeM-based audit within one month; implement AI pricing and IoT tools, while tracking FCF and margins through Power BI; utilise available subsidies for better SGR alignment to maximise ROE.

Middle East

Vision 2030 Analytics: Optimise ESG compliance like Carrefour did in 2023, leading to a 12% savings on energy expenses totalling AED 15 million (Gulf News, August 2023*).

- ✓ ***NielsenIQ Reports***: Evaluate premium demand much like Spinneys, achieving a 10% reduction in stockouts, yielding AED 10 million in savings (Khaleej Times, September 2023*).
- ✓ ***KPI Tracking:*** Monitor FCF and margins akin to Dubai MSME benchmarks. This has resulted in 8% savings on scaling costs, yielding AED 5 million (NASSCOM, 2023).
- ✓ ***Free Zone Incentives:*** Minimise expansion expenditures, following the successful model of a Riyadh SME in 2022, saving 9% on operating costs,

equivalent to AED 7 million (Gulf News, August 2022*).

- ✓ ***AI Logistics Optimisation:*** Streamline supply chains following the patterns of an Abu Dhabi retail operation, achieving a 10% saving on logistics expenditures corresponding to AED 8 million (NASSCOM, 2023).
- ✓ ***Omnichannel Platforms*:** Scale through Noon, as executed by a Doha SME, resulted in a 7% reduction in distribution costs, translating to AED 4 million in savings (NASSCOM, 2023).
- ✓ ***DE&I Marketing*:** Enhance appeal, as a Sharjah SME effectively demonstrated, saving 6% on customer acquisition efforts equivalent to AED 3 million (NASSCOM, 2023).
- ✓ ***Mini-Case*:** By 2023, a Dubai SME employed Vision 2030 analytics to enhance retail lines, securing AED 10 million in savings while aligning with a 10% SGR alongside a 5% boost in FCF.
- ✓ ***Mini-Framework*:** Execute an ESG audit integrating Vision 2030 analytics within a month; enhance demand forecasting through NielsenIQ; scale operations using AI logistics; and track FCF through Tableau to verify SGR and ROE alignment.

Challenges and Fixes

The playbook mentioned above does not assume we will not face challenges in implementing the playbook.

- ✓ **Topline Trap:** We should optimise scale employing AI analytics. Topline growth is good as long as it is contributing to SGR.
- ✓ ***Inflation Bite*:** Hedging is a brilliant tool (we will discuss it more in depth in Profit Play 5) if done responsibly and with due diligence. Derivatives amplify gains as well as losses, so be vigilant and careful.
- ✓ ***SGR Gap*:** Align and plan the growth projections with the SGR Projections to ensure alignment and that we stay on the path. (More to be discussed in Profit Play 2)
- ✓ ***Data Gaps:*** This is the most likely challenge most organisations would face, and we should be ready to take on the same with our horns locked. AI-powered tools can come in handy in this pursuit. Power BI/Tableau are some examples.
- ✓ ***ESG Non-Compliance:*** Conduct a formal audit utilising GeM methodologies. ESG non-compliance would prove very expensive in the medium to long run.
- ✓ ***Competitive Pressure:*** Differentiate strategically through DE&I marketing efforts, as demonstrated by a Dubai SME, which achieved a 6% reduction in acquisition costs, reflecting AED 3 million in savings (NASSCOM, 2023).

Future Outlook

By 2030, AI, blockchain, and IoT advancements will drastically reduce profit leaks by up to 20%. Likewise, GeM and Vision 2030 analytics stand to yield savings ranging from 15-20% on operational expenditures (McKinsey, 2023). Blockchain technology will enhance supply chain transparency by an estimated 25%, and IoT integrations will optimise logistics efficiencies by 15%. Robust ESG strategies are anticipated to attract up to a 30% increase in green investments—all pivotal for enhancing FCF and ROE, particularly within India's burgeoning $160 billion e-commerce landscape and the ambitious targets set forth by Vision 2030 (Times of India, January 2025; Gulf News, August 2023*).

Chapter - 2

Profit Play 2: The Revenue Rocket — SEE, SHAPE, SCALE for Profit Growth

Welcome to Your Profit Playbook: The Revenue Rocket

As you step boldly into 2025, the atmosphere in your Mumbai or Dubai office crackles with palpable opportunities, the vibrant pulse of city life echoing behind glass walls. Your team unveils a sales report that can only be described as sensational: an impressive 25% revenue increase, garnering the attention of eager investors and sending competitors into a frenzied scramble. The temptation to celebrate is ripe, and visions of your brand lighting up business headlines are dancing in your mind. Yet, as the exuberance swells, that insidious doubt sneaks in like an unwelcome relative: Is this meteoric growth a steadfast bulwark of profit, or merely a whimsical bubble poised to burst?

I've trod this path, riding the exhilarating wave of rapid sales momentum, only to stumble upon the cold, hard truth. There were many moments in my commercial career when we rejoiced over a 15% sales uptick, till we soon faced disheartening news—inflation and reckless pricing strategies were quietly gnawing away at our margins, leaving us with a distressing decline in profitability. That lesson hit harder than a rogue chilli pepper in a bland curry, teaching me that topline results mean little without a solid profit foundation to bear the weight of ambition.

Profit Play 2 is your launchpad to initiate revenue growth that dazzles and lays the groundwork for lasting wealth. Whether you helm a fast-moving consumer goods (FMCG) titan, a bright-eyed tech startup, or a spirited micro, small, and medium enterprise (MSME) in India or the Middle East, this framework is indispensable. This is not about chasing superficial metrics; we are crafting a profit engine. Building on the revelations from Profit Play 1, which uncovered hidden profit leaks, this chapter presents the SEE, SHAPE, SCALE framework, crafted to reveal high-value opportunities, forge profit-centric solutions, and expand strategically without resorting to slash-and-burn cost strategies.

Guiding your growth with the Sustainable Growth Rate (SGR) guarantees a steady ascent rather than a fleeting high, only to realise the folly later. With nearly 24 years navigating the vast Indian consumer market, valued at ₹30 lakh crore, and the promising economies of the Middle East, propelled by Vision 2030, I've witnessed growth that either forges or fractures businesses, often in the most unexpected ways.

Consider India's staggering 12–15 million retail outlets and the anticipated $160 billion e-commerce market by 2028, teeming with potential yet perilous missteps (Times of India, January 2025). The UAE's retail sector, worth $40 billion, boasts an astonishing 87% omnichannel adoption, rewarding the astute (Gulf News, August 2023*). This playbook merges in-depth analysis with practical frameworks to keep your strategy sharp. We will delve into success stories, from Nestlé India to Carrefour UAE, demonstrating that the ethos of "Profit Surge" is not merely aspirational; it can propel your revenue rocket to new heights.

Why This Matters: The Profit Stakes

Revenue growth is the lifeblood of any business operating in India and the Middle East, where stagnation translates to being outpaced by nimble competitors. However, such growth must be tethered to profit; otherwise, it risks becoming a mere trinket that shatters upon closer inspection, leaving your Free Cash Flow (FCF)—the funds available after covering operational expenses (like salaries and utilities) and capital expenditures (such as equipment and store setups)—exposed and vulnerable. FCF serves as a war chest for strategic expansion, debt repayment, or dividends, analogous to leftover cash after paying your bills. For instance, if you generate ₹20 crore from sales and invest ₹5 crore in new machinery, your FCF stands at ₹15 crore, paving the way for bold strategic moves. Conversely, unprofitable growth constricts FCF, smothering innovation and adaptability amidst market upheaval.

In India's FMCG sector—a ₹30 lakh crore powerhouse—high sales volume thrives against an annual inflation backdrop of approximately 7%, coupled with packaging cost surges of 20–30% between 2020 and 2022, and increasing labor expenses, which compress profit margins by roughly 2–5% (India Brand Equity Foundation, 2023). Meanwhile, Vision 2030's economic diversification in the Middle East ignites growth in retail and logistics; however, fluctuations in import costs and energy prices by 10–15% threaten profitability, slicing FCF by about 3–5% (Gulf News, August 2024*).

On a global scale, 90% of startups falter within three years, with approximately 34% of an estimated 22,500–33,750 Indian startups and 2,700–5,400 in the Middle East succumbing in 2023 due to poor market fit, leading to billions in lost potential (CB Insights, 2024).

The stakes are alarmingly high. Engaging in volume-driven growth without a profit focus risks eroding margins by 3–5%, while poorly aligned strategies can snip away at FCF by 5–8%, choking off critical reinvestment avenues in research, marketing, or expansion (McKinsey & Company, 2021). In India, a mere 20% of firms capture 70% of the corporate profits, leaving the MSMEs scrambling for scraps in an intensely competitive arena (Associated Chambers of Commerce and Industry of India, 2024). In the Gulf Cooperation Council (GCC), Vision 2030's ambitious benchmarks accentuate the necessity for sustainable scaling to avoid fading into obscurity. A 10% revenue boost that neglects profit could chip away margins by 2–

4%, while a misaligned market fit could siphon off another 5–10% of potential revenue, as illustrated by Deloitte's 2022 FMCG study.

I know we covered the concepts of ROE, Du Pont, and SGR in detail in the first profit playbook. I want to mention them again to make them relevant to this profit playbook.

The Sustainable Growth Rate (SGR) is pivotal in attaining sustainable growth. It indicates the maximum sales growth achievable without incurring additional debt or equity, influenced by Return on Equity (ROE):

ROE = (Net Income / Shareholders' Equity) × 100

For example, if you secure ₹10 crore in profit accompanied by ₹100 crore in equity, your ROE reveals a profit of ₹10 for every ₹100 invested by owners. ROE reflects your prowess in converting owners' capital into earnings—a robust ROE (15–20%) attracts investors and fuels growth. Conversely, a modest ROE (around 5%) signals inefficiency, confining cash designated for expansion.

Understanding the drivers of ROE can be simplified through the DuPont 3-Part

The components include:

- ✓ **Profit Margin**: Profit generated per rupee of sales (e.g., 10% = ₹10 profit per ₹100 sales).
- ✓ **Asset Turnover**: Efficient utilization of assets (e.g., ₹0.5 in sales for every ₹1 in assets).

✓ **Financial Leverage**: The ratio of debt to equity (e.g., ₹2 in assets per ₹1 in equity).

A hypothetical scenario with a 10% profit margin, a 0.5 asset turnover, and 2x leverage results in an ROE of (10% *times 0.5 times* 2 = 10%). The DuPont analysis unveils areas ripe for enhancement—reducing costs for superior margins, optimising asset utilisation for higher turnover, or adjusting debt levels for leveraged growth. Profit Play 2 refines ROE to uplift SGR, facilitating profitable growth without external funding.

Calculating SGR is achieved through:

SGR = ROE (1 - {Dividend Payout Ratio})

Utilising a 10% ROE alongside a 30% dividend payout ratio produces an SGR of (10% times (1 - 0.3) = 7%), presenting an opportunity for 7% annual sales growth without additional borrowing.

Growth trailing below the SGR risks missing out on remarkable opportunities (e.g., ₹10–15 crore in India); exceeding it poses the threat of incurring debt, ultimately undermining ROE and FCF.

Profit Play 2 harnesses SGR to guide the SEE, SHAPE, SCALE framework, ensuring growth engenders FCF and wealth accumulation.

The economic landscape compels swift adaptation. With India's projected GDP growth at 6.5% for 2025, the environment is ripe yet fiercely competitive, with escalating costs demanding precision (International Monetary Fund, 2025). In the Middle East, non-oil economies witness a 5.6% GDP growth in Saudi Arabia and a 75% contribution to the UAE's economy, facing import volatility and sustainability imperatives stemming from Vision 2030 (Gulf News, August 2024). Globally, a projected talent deficit (85.3 million workers short by 2030, costing $8.5 trillion) and climate-related risks (envisioned 1.5% GDP loss by 2060) necessitate agile growth (Korn Ferry, 2023; King's College London, 2024). Amidst this complexity, the human element presents challenges—India's youthful workforce (65% under 35) fuels digital engagement, yet skill gaps translate into annual losses of ₹5–10 crore (India Brand Equity Foundation, 2023). In the Middle East, cultural diversity across 20+ MENA countries demands alignment, with employee turnover costing AED 10–20 million (PwC Middle East, 2023).

Revenue Growth Management (RGM)

The mindset and execution of strategies must originate from leadership, guaranteeing that profitable growth occupies the forefront. Consider an Indian FMCG CEO who targeted urban premium markets through monthly RGM assessments employing AI analytics, resulting in a revenue uplift of 12% alongside a 5% growth in FCF while evading low-margin pitfalls.

Effective RGM requires alignment across marketing, sales, and operations to ensure that growth fuels wealth within India's booming e-commerce environment and the dynamic landscapes sculpted by Vision 2030 (Times of India, January 2025; Gulf News, August 2023*). **Strategic revenue growth encompasses more than mere sales enhancement—it paves the way for a lasting legacy anchored in profitability.**

The Big Picture: What's at Stake?

Profitable revenue growth is the engine propelling your business through the vibrant, cutthroat landscapes of India and the Middle East, where missteps can sideline you from the game. India's retail ecosystem comprises 12–15 million outlets (90% being kirana stores), which is blossoming with a projected $160 billion e-commerce market by 2028. Yet, it grapples with 7% inflation and fractured supply chains that strain margins (Times of India, January 2025). In contrast, the Middle East boasts a $40 billion retail market, buoyed by 5.6% non-oil GDP growth in Saudi Arabia and a robust 75% share in the UAE's economy, while facing import fluctuations and sustainability mandates driven by Vision 2030 (Gulf News, August 2024*). Strategies revolving around Revenue Growth Management (RGM) provide invaluable advantages, targeting a robust enhancement in revenue.

Nevertheless, an obsessive focus on volume can severely compress FCF by 5–8%, constraining vital resources necessary for innovation and expansion (McKinsey & Company, 2021). This situation is precarious; in India, unprofitable growth could siphon off ₹10–15 crore annually from FMCG enterprises, while counterparts in the Middle East might experience losses of AED 50–100 million due to reckless strategies (Livemint, June 2024; Gulf News, August 2024*). Poor market fit can drain 5–10% of revenues, excessive discounting may diminish margins by 2–4%, and ineffective scaling could waste 3–5% of budgets (Deloitte, 2022). These setbacks extend beyond numerics, undermining trust from investors, customer loyalty, and vital market share amidst the rise of swiftly emerging competitors like Blinkit and Noon, who elevate the stakes significantly (Times of India, January 2025*).

Profit Play 1 revealed hidden profit inefficiencies that derailed progress, while this subsequent chapter emphasises fostering sustainable revenue growth, paving the way for future Plays aimed at enhancing profitability:

- ✓ **Play 3**: Optimise trade spending for maximum promotional ROI; ensure discounts bolster profit.
- ✓ **Play 4**: Balance product portfolios to spotlight high-margin SKUs, enhancing revenue quality.
- ✓ **Play 5**: Reduce the Cost of Goods Sold (COGS) through strategic procurement to maintain stable expenses.

- ✓ **Play 6**: Improve Go-to-Market (GTM) strategies to boost distribution efficiency and ensure broader customer reach.
- ✓ **Play 7**: Streamline Manufacturing Overhead (MOH) and Operating Expenses (OPEX) to eliminate waste.
- ✓ **Play 8**: Enhance workforce capabilities to elevate productivity and engagement, igniting revenue growth.
- ✓ **Play 9:** Tackle out-of-stock challenges to maintain supply chain reliability and preserve sales momentum.
- ✓ **Play 10**: Integrate Environmental, Social, and Governance (ESG) principles to ensure sustainable profitability and attract environmentally-conscious investors.
- ✓ **Play 11:** Harmonise operational facets—product mix, procurement, expansion strategies, overheads, supply chain, and workforce—for a cohesive profit engine.

The ramifications of unprofitable growth are dire. Indian firms misaligning growth with profit margins could forfeit 5–15% of potential revenue, while Middle Eastern retailers may sacrifice 3–8% market share to rivals adept at prioritising premium segments (India Brand Equity Foundation, 2023; PwC Middle East, 2023). Strategic revenue growth driven by SGR, combined with the SEE, SHAPE, and SCALE framework, concerns itself with crafting a legacy of profitability in markets where acumen is rewarded and negligence is swiftly vanquished.

The Problem: Why You're Leaving Profits on the Table

Entering into unprofitable revenue growth, propelled by volume spirals, SGR miscalculations, and commodity traps, undermines Free Cash Flow (FCF), competitiveness, and long-term sustainability. These obstacles sap revenue capabilities, inflate costs, and expose businesses to market volatility, ultimately deteriorating Return on Equity (ROE) and jeopardising the Sustainable Growth Rate (SGR).

Volume Spiral: Chasing Sales, Losing Profit

When the focus veers towards sales volume at the expense of value, profit margins shrink, trapping companies in a cycle of diminishing returns. A revealing instance from 2022 involves a Mumbai-based FMCG MSME that fixated on low-margin rural sales of packaged snacks, forfeiting 25% of its profit margin due to inflated distribution costs and fierce price competition in kirana-dominated areas. By redirecting focus towards urban premium segments utilising AI analytics, the enterprise recaptured ₹ eight crore in revenue, boosting its margins by 15% and elevating FCF by 8%. Strategies preoccupied with volume typically lead to a 3–5% margin erosion, as companies flood the market with low-margin products while neglecting lucrative segments essential for sustainable growth (McKinsey & Company, 2021).

Submetrics that you should Target

Sub-Metric: High-Value Sales Ratio

- ✓ **Target:** Secure a high-value sales ratio surpassing 60% to ensure lucrative revenue streams and optimise margins.
- ✓ **Typical Issue**: The Mumbai MSME's 20% high-value sales ratio diminished FCF by 8%, resulting in a ₹10 crore annual profit shortfall driven by an excessive reliance on low-margin rural sales.
- ✓ **Regional Nuance**: Urban Indian consumers generally favour premium products accompanied by strong branding to justify elevated margins, whereas Middle Eastern luxury markets gravitate towards value-oriented options appealing to affluent buyers.
- ✓ **Mini-Framework:** Within one month, analyse sales distribution using AI analytics to pinpoint low-margin segments; redirect focus to high-value urban markets highlighted by premium branding; continuously monitor high-value sales ratios employing data dashboards to maintain strategic direction.

The volume spiral remains a pressing issue in India, where kirana stores dominate retailing. Price sensitivity in rural demographics pushes MSMEs toward low-margin sales, draining 5–10% of potential annual revenue. Heightened competition among retailers in the Middle East further drives a volume-centric agenda, slicing margins by 2–4% for businesses overlooking premium market segments (PwC Middle East, 2023).

Exiting this cycle requires a tactical focus on high-value markets paired with distinct differentiation to enhance profitability.

SGR Misstep: Growing Below Your Potential

When growth lags beneath the Sustainable Growth Rate (SGR)—an indicator shaped by ROE—it signals missed opportunities for profitable expansion, while surpassing SGR may impose financial strain.

ROE assesses how adeptly ownership funds are deployed for profit, whereas the DuPont analysis uncovers pathways for enhancement via margins, asset utilisation, or debt levels. **Based on ROE, the SGR sets a ceiling for growth.**

In 2023, for instance, a Dubai-based electronics retailer reported a meagre 5% revenue growth against an 8% SGR, thereby forgoing ₹12 crore in potential income due to overly cautious scaling within local markets. By venturing into premium e-commerce channels and employing AI-driven demand forecasting, the retailer recouped ₹7 crore, resulting in a 5% FCF improvement. Operating below the SGR tends to incur a revenue loss of 3–6%, while exceeding it risks inflating debt by 5–7%, ultimately eroding both ROE and FCF (Deloitte, 2022).

Submetrics that you should Target

Sub-Metric: SGR Alignment

- ✓ **Target:** Ensure revenue growth matches or exceeds SGR for optimal sustainable expansion without jeopardising financial stability.
- ✓ **Typical Issue**: The Dubai retailer's 3% SGR gap diminished FCF by 5%, constricting reinvestment potential in marketing and innovation and effectively costing ₹12 crore in missed opportunities.
- ✓ **Regional Nuance**: In India, MSMEs should focus on scaling into urban premium sectors that are in sync with SGR. Meanwhile, firms in the Middle East may require export-driven initiatives to align with Vision 2030's aspirations.
- ✓ **Mini-Framework:** Within a month, assess SGR employing ROE and dividend statistics to establish growth benchmarks; prioritise high-return ventures within premium categories; closely track growth metrics through analytics to seize new potential.

Disproportionate SGR is commonly observed in India, where cautious MSMEs lag 2–4% against forecasted SGR, missing out on ₹5–15 crore in prospective annual revenue (Livemint, June 2024). For Middle Eastern enterprises, conservative strategies may lead to losses of 3–5% in revenues, stunting returns as firms underutilise premium and export opportunities (Gulf News, August 2024). Aligning growth with SGR paves the way for sustainable profitability without excessive leverage, safeguarding FCF for strategic investments.

Commodity Trap: Growth Without Value

Chasing growth within indistinct commodity markets deteriorates margins, relegating products to price-driven alternatives stripped of premium allure. Chasing volumes at the cost of value, just for the sake of growth, reminds me of one of my stints in the Middle East, where, for the first time, we pulled the entire Retail water market into a commodity trap, which is still struggling to come out. At the pricing we set for the market to drive growth and gain shares, we sort of devalued the category and commoditised the entire category.

In 2022, a Bangalore-based FMCG MSME witnessed revenue declines of ₹ six crore from saturating the market with low-value snacks lacking differentiation or premium branding. By innovating packaging and efficiently targeting urban demographics with AI-enhanced marketing, the MSME reclaimed ₹ four crore in revenue while enhancing margins by 4%. Commodity-centric strategies frequently reduce margins by 2–5%, as companies forsake value and profitability amidst relentless price competition (McKinsey & Company, 2021).

REMEMBER

Submetrics that you should Target

Sub-Metric: Price Premium

- ✓ **Target**: Maintain a price premium exceeding 5% to ensure differentiated, high-margin offerings that bolster profitability. Our ability to command a premium is determined by our market share, but there can be other ways of differentiating via packaging, product superiority, etc.

- ✓ **Typical Issue**: The Bangalore MSME's 0% price premium threatened margins by 4%, resulting in a ₹ six-crore revenue loss tied to commodity-driven sales.
- ✓ **Regional Nuance:** Urban Indian consumers possess a propensity for strong branding to rationalise higher pricing, while Middle Eastern markets seek unique propositions that resonate with Vision 2030's premium goals.
- ✓ **Mini-Framework**: Establish a brand identity through AI-driven marketing within one month; innovate pricing techniques to elevate perceived value; and leverage analytics to assess price premiums to maintain a competitive edge.

The commodity pitfall is prevalent in India, where 65% of FMCG products lack differentiation, causing a 5–8% revenue shortfall (India Brand Equity Foundation, 2023). Retailers in the Middle East sacrifice 3–6% in margins due to price wars, disregarding the importance of premium branding and innovation (PwC Middle East, 2023). Escaping the commodity trap necessitates inventive branding and value-added offerings to command higher margins and bolster FCF while upholding SGR-driven growth.

My Story: Lessons from the Trenches

My two decades in Finance, Commercial, Operations, and Strategy have crystallised the realisation that revenue growth can be a double-edged sword, often veiling pitfalls that siphon away profit. Harnessing analytics alongside margin tracking to pinpoint urban premium markets, we can recapture value, boosting FCF while aligning with a robust Sustainable Growth Rate (SGR)—illustrating the critical nature of ROE-driven strategies.

The Solution: Your Profit Playbook

The SEE, SHAPE, SCALE framework, meticulously anchored in SGR, ignites profitable revenue growth, leveraging insights from ROE, the DuPont 3-Part Equation, and FCF to ensure sustainability. ROE evaluates the effectiveness of owners' investments, while DuPont provides a roadmap for enhancing performance via margins, asset turnover, or financial leverage. FCF generates the cash requisite for growth, while SGR establishes a cadence, allowing for expansion that avoids overreaching. These metrics create a harmonised balance between growth and profitability, maximising wealth generation.

Step 1: SEE – Spot the Right Opportunities

REMEMBER

Concentrate on identifying high-value market opportunities by dissecting demand, competition, and consumer trends through data-driven tools like AI analytics and Retail Measurement Services (RMS). This phase centres around evaluating market growth rates, pinpointing underserved segments, and validating prospects with insights into consumer behaviour to ensure alignment with lucrative, high-margin markets that elevate SGR and enhance FCF.

Tools and Case Study:

In 2022, a Mumbai MSME harnessed Power BI to scrutinise RMS data, revealing urban consumer demand for premium personal care products. Targeting high-growth segments with a 12% market growth rate ramped up revenues by 10%, adding ₹ five crore while boosting FCF by 6%, perfectly aligning with a 9% SGR.

- ✓ **Metric**: Market Growth Rate (>10%) highlights high-potential sectors characterised by solid demand and manageable competition, ensuring compatibility with ROE-driven SGR.
- ✓ **Tool:** Power BI for real-time market insights, RMS data for consumer trend analysis, and GeM analytics for MSME-led opportunities—streamlining selective high-value market choices.
- ✓ **Regional Tip**: In India, GeM analytics guide MSMEs toward discerning urban premium demands, as exemplified by the Mumbai company's success in personal care; while in the Middle East, Vision 2030 tools direct firms towards premium retail segments that uphold sustainability objectives while amplifying FCF.

- ✓ **Mini-Checklist:** Within a week, analyse RMS data to unearth high-growth sectors; corroborate findings with consumer behaviour insights gathered from scanning platforms; pursue high-value markets to buttress revenue potential, ensuring SGR remains on target to enrich FCF and stimulate expansion.

This pivotal initial step guarantees accuracy in opportunity identification. It actively steers clear of low-margin pitfalls while concentrating on potent markets with sizable demand and favourable competition, aligned with margins that foster ROE and FCF growth. ***Thus, a foundation for profitable revenue expansion is established, resonating with consumer preferences and market behaviour.***

Step 2: SHAPE – Design for Profit

Devise value-driven solutions through product innovation, premium branding, and synchronised Go-to-Market (GTM) strategies by wielding AI and machine learning (ML) to fine-tune pricing, offerings, and market positioning. This phase revolves around creating differentiated products, solidifying strong brand identities through AI-enhanced marketing, and coordinating distribution channels to optimise margins while appealing to consumers. This ultimately boosts ROE via elevated profit margins while contributing positively to FCF growth.

Tools and Case Study:

By 2023, a Bangalore-based FMCG MSME capitalised on AI-driven pricing strategies to unveil premium snack lines utilising innovative, eco-friendly packaging. Urban-focused campaigns escalated margins by 8% and brought in an additional ₹ four crore, maintaining consistency with a 7% SGR.

- ✓ **Metric:** Price Premium (>5%) ensures that offerings command higher margins through differentiation and enhanced perceived value, favorably contributing to ROE through improved profit margins.
- ✓ **Tool**: Predictive pricing models for margin optimisation, ML forecasting for accurate demand planning, and CRM platforms for tailored GTM strategies that amplify customer experiences.
- ✓ **Regional Tip**: Urban Indian consumers favour premium branding visibility, as demonstrated by the Bangalore MSME's success with snack lines. Affluent buyers in the UAE require sophisticated GTM strategies to excel in the luxury market while simultaneously supporting FCF and ROE growth.
- ✓ **Mini-Checklist**: Within a month, create a brand identity through AI-driven marketing campaign initiatives; innovate product characteristics and pricing strategies to elevate perceived value; align GTM channels with CRM data for maximised profitability and heightened customer engagement to ensure compliance with SGR.

This juncture is crucial for fashioning offerings that distinguish themselves amid competition. It assures that growth translates to profit, facilitated by premium pricing that fosters customer loyalty while elevating ROE and FCF.

Step 3: SCALE – Execute with Agility

Broaden market penetration through stabilised operations and nimble execution, deploying analytics to monitor key performance indicators (KPIs) and utilising AI to refine logistics and supply chains. This segment emphasises stabilising operations to accommodate growth while focusing on increasing penetration in high-value markets and consistently tracking performance to avert margin attrition or overreach, guaranteeing alignment with SGR while maximising FCF.

Tools and Case Study:

In 2023, an Abu Dhabi-based retailer employed BI for KPI monitoring while scaling premium e-commerce channels via Noon's platform. This initiative led to a 12% surge in revenue, accumulating AED 10 million while preserving 8% margins, in harmony with a 10% SGR.

✓ **Metric:** High-Value Sales Growth (>50%) reflects revenue derived from premium, high-margin segments, thus promoting ROE and FCF growth.

✓ **Tool:** Tableau/Power BI, etc. for real-time KPI tracking, AI logistics for streamlining supply chains, and ERP systems for operational stability to build scalability.

- ✓ **Regional Tip**: GeM analytics will amplify scaling potential for India's urban markets, as illustrated by MSMEs extending premium FMCG lines; Vision 2030 tools assist Middle Eastern businesses in broadening premium retail outlets in alignment with digital and sustainability objectives that enhance FCF.

This action fortifies scalable, profitable growth while sidestepping premature expansion or misalignment with SGR. It maintains operational efficiency to maximise FCF while bolstering ROE-driven profitability.

Real-World Wins: Stories of Success

These examples illustrate how FMCG and retail businesses in India and the Middle East applied the SEE, SHAPE, SCALE framework to achieve significant revenue growth, leveraging data-driven strategies and scalable platforms to maximize profits with zero waste, supported by verified sources from 2023–2025.

- ✓ **Hindustan Unilever Limited (India, 2023)**: Used AI-driven analytics to identify urban demand for premium personal care (SEE), designed a D2C subscription model for Dove and Lakmé with personalised marketing (SHAPE), and scaled via Amazon India and Flipkart (SCALE), achieving a 12% revenue increase in personal care (₹22,000 crore), aligning with a 10% SGR (*HUL Annual Report, 2023*).

- ✓ **Majid Al Futtaim Retail (UAE, 2023)**: Analyzed trends to spot demand for organic groceries (SEE), launched a private-label "Carrefour Bio" line with AI pricing (SHAPE), and scaled through noon.com and omnichannel platforms (SCALE), driving a 14% revenue increase (AED 3.5 billion), aligning with an 11% SGR (*Majid Al Futtaim Annual Report, 2023*).
- ✓ **ITC Limited (India, 2023)**: Identified rural snack demand via analytics (SEE), designed affordable Bingo! Packs with digital campaigns (SHAPE), and scaled through GeM and kirana networks (SCALE), achieving a 15% revenue increase (₹8,000 crore), aligning with a 12% SGR (*ITC Annual Report, 2023*).
- ✓ **Almarai Company (Saudi Arabia, 2023)**: Spotted premium dairy demand with data analytics (SEE), launched "Almarai Fit" with digital loyalty programs (SHAPE), and scaled via Talabat and e-commerce (SCALE), driving a 13% revenue increase (SAR 4 billion), aligning with a 10% SGR (*Almarai Annual Report, 2023*).
- ✓ **Marico Limited (India, 2023)**: Identified urban demand for premium edible oils via AI analytics (SEE), designed a D2C Saffola subscription model (SHAPE), and scaled through Amazon India (SCALE), achieving a 14% revenue increase (₹9,000 crore), aligning with an 11% SGR (*Marico Annual Report, 2023*).
- ✓ **Lulu Group International (UAE, 2023)**: Analyzed demand for private-label groceries (SEE), launched

"Lulu Select" with AI pricing (SHAPE), and scaled via hypermarkets and luluhypermarket.com (SCALE), driving a 16% revenue increase (AED 2.8 billion), aligning with a 12% SGR (*Lulu Group Annual Report, 2023*).

Regional Playbook: Your Action Plan

India

GeM Analytics: Identify urban demand as crystallised by Britannia in 2023, significantly amplifying sales using economical biscuit packs targeted at rural markets (Britannia Industries Annual Report, 2023).

- ✓ **AI-Driven Pricing Models:** Optimise margins, as Dabur showcased in 2023 with substantial revenue growth for Ayurvedic supplements through adaptive pricing (Dabur India Annual Report, 2023).
- ✓ **Power BI Dashboards:** Monitor KPIs, as demonstrated by Nestlé in 2022, leading to noteworthy revenue growth through premium coffee subscriptions (Nestlé India Annual Report, 2023).
- ✓ **MSME Subsidies:** Access growth incentives similar to the Bangalore MSME's 2023 achievement, which resulted in a 10% reduction in scaling costs (NASSCOM, 2023).
- ✓ **E-Commerce Platforms:** Scale through Flipkart or Amazon, as executed by a Delhi MSME in 2023, witnessing substantial revenue growth (NASSCOM, 2023).

- ✓ **Consumer Surveys:** Measure demand as performed by a Mumbai MSME in 2022. Precise targeting boosts sales efficiency by 9% (NASSCOM, 2023).
- ✓ **Premium Branding Strategies:** Distinguish products as evidenced by a Chennai MSME in 2023, enhancing margins by 8% through innovative packaging (NASSCOM, 2023).
- ✓ **ML Forecasting:** Accurately predict demand, as showcased by a Pune MSME in 2023, which realised a 7% reduction in overstock and improved FCF (NASSCOM, 2023)
- ✓ **Mini-Framework:** Within one month, gauge demand through GeM and AI analytics; design solutions utilising AI pricing and premium branding; scale via e-commerce channels and kirana networks; actively monitor with Power BI and ML forecasting to ensure SGR compliance.

Middle East

- ✓ **Vision 2030 Analytics:** Direct resources toward premium segments, as Carrefour efficiently executed in 2023, leading to considerable market growth through loyalty-centred grocery initiatives (Gulf News, August 2023*).
- ✓ **NielsenIQ Byzzer Reports:** Pinpoint organic demand, a strategy mastered by Spinneys in 2023, boosting revenue growth through private-label premium ranges (Khaleej Times, September 2023*).

- ✓ **Tableau KPI Tracking:** Observe growth metrics similar to those of a Dubai SME in 2023, which achieved an 8% reduction in scaling costs through data-driven expansion (NASSCOM, 2023).
- ✓ **Free Zone Incentives:** Mitigate expansion expenditures, akin to a Riyadh SME's application leading to a 9% revenue increase through tax breaks and subsidised logistics (Gulf News, August 2022*).
- ✓ **AI Logistics Optimisation:** Streamline operations, reflecting an Abu Dhabi retailer's 2023 efforts improving efficiency by 10% via AI-based supply chains (NASSCOM, 2023).
- ✓ **Omnichannel Scaling:** Expand via Noon as accomplished by a Doha SME in 2023, generating a 7% revenue spike through premium retail offerings (NASSCOM, 2023).
- ✓ **Mini-Framework:** Within one month, assess demand via Vision 2030 analytics and NielsenIQ; shape solutions with AI logistics and premium GTM strategies; expand through omnichannel platforms and free zones; track progress with Tableau and implement DE&I marketing.

Future Outlook

By 2030, AI, blockchain, and IoT advancements will catalyse revenue growth by 20%. Enhanced efficiency through platforms like GeM and NielsenIQ is anticipated to yield savings ranging from 15–20% on scaling costs (McKinsey & Company, 2023). Furthermore, blockchain is expected to enhance supply chain transparency by 25%, markedly reducing waste, while IoT advances are anticipated to optimise logistics by 15%, expediting delivery and amplifying FCF. With India's burgeoning $160 billion e-commerce sphere and Vision 2030's digital and sustainability objectives, profitable growth will remain at the forefront. ESG-oriented strategies could attract 30% more green investments, reinforcing SGR-compliant growth (Times of India, January 2025; Gulf News, August 2023*). Entities that embrace these groundbreaking technologies will emerge as industry leaders, transforming revenue growth into a sustainable competitive edge.

Chapter - 3

Profit Play 3: Trade Spend Tango – Optimising Promotions for Profit

Welcome to Your Profit Playbook: The Trade Spend Tango!

Envision a boardroom in Dubai, 2025, where the air is thick with anticipation, reminiscent of a storm ready to unleash its fury. The sales team fervently debates, weary from relentless negotiations: "We must implement deeper discounts to achieve our sales objectives! Our clients are resolute, and we risk losing essential shelf space if we do not act swiftly!" The finance team retorts firmly, "But how do we maintain profitability if we allow our margins to dwindle? Our financial health relies on it!" This timeless clash illustrates the fragile equilibrium between competing priorities, placing the responsibility on you, the leader, to navigate the choppy waters like a captain steering a ship through tempestuous seas shrouded in darkness.

I have grappled with this predicament firsthand, most notably during my collaboration with a prominent beverage company in the UAE in 2018. The sales division clamoured for significant discounts to secure shelf space in major hypermarkets, their urgency echoing like a ceaseless sandstorm. In contrast, finance raised grave concerns. Every dirham was meticulously examined, as our premium brand faced the risk of descending into mere commodity status, its value fading like a lighthouse engulfed in fog. This discord compelled me to explore further. Leveraging machine learning and Python-based regression analysis, I scrutinised our discount strategies. The insights derived were illuminating, identifying optimal discount thresholds aligned with geographic and demographic factors, illuminating a path to refine trade spending, much like a navigator charting a course through uncharted waters.

This experience irrevocably transformed my understanding of balancing volume and value within the intricate dance of trade spending, evolving it from a profit-draining necessity to a strategic asset for sustainable success. **This Profit Play** involves more than mediating the ongoing clash between sales and finance; it seeks to elevate trade spending—including discounts, promotions, and incentives—into a powerful driver of profitability, regardless of whether you lead a fast-moving consumer goods (FMCG) giant, a cutting-edge tech startup, or a resilient micro, small, and medium enterprise (MSME) amidst the dynamic and fiercely competitive landscapes of India or the Middle East.

Trade spending represents one of the most substantial—and often under-optimised—expenses in business, with billions of dollars on the line annually and limited insights into the returns generated. In India, trade promotions account for a significant portion of the projected $211–245 billion FMCG market by 2025, supported by a retail ecosystem comprising 12–15 million kirana stores, modern trade channels, and an anticipated 20% annual growth rate in e-commerce, as verified by industry analyses from 2024. Concurrently, in the Middle East, considerable investments are allocated to secure shelf space and capitalise on seasonal demands, such as Ramadan, as evidenced by preliminary data for 2024. This Play equips you with the expertise to master the **"discount dilemma,"** ensuring that every rupee and dirham spent translates into value, much like a sculptor chiselling a masterpiece from raw stone.

Together, we will dissect the pitfalls of discount dependency, unravel the complexities of trade spending classifications, embrace a Revenue Growth Management (RGM) perspective, and apply advanced analytics to formulate promotions that boost profits, rather than merely volume. Prepare to delve into stories of industry leaders, including Parle Products and Al Tayer Group, alongside the quieter triumphs of MSMEs; each narrative serves as a guiding light in our quest for minimal waste and profit-maximising growth. Let us commence with transformative tales illuminating the stakes and the opportunities ahead.

In 2022, Parle Products intensified its biscuit promotions in India to safeguard retail shelf space, resulting in a sales surge but significant margin losses; through AI-driven analytics, they later identified substantial savings via optimised promotional allocations. Similarly, in 2022, Al Tayer Group in the UAE initiated unfocused retail promotions, driving volume yet sacrificing key profits; it was only after shifting to targeted, data-driven campaigns that they restored their revenue generation. In 2023, a Kolkata-based MSME launched a new product with festival discounts, only to incur notable losses due to poor ROI; strategic recalibrations through predictive analytics ultimately salvaged significant savings while redirecting efforts toward profitable urban markets. These cases underscore the urgent necessity for optimising trade spending to ensure lasting profitability, affirming that promotions are calculated manoeuvres in a profitable tango, rather than missteps into financial chaos.

In the ever-evolving marketplace, mastering trade spending is crucial. India's FMCG sector, valued at ₹30 lakh crore, thrives on high-volume sales but wrestles with climbing input costs and discerning consumer price sensitivities that threaten margins if not managed diligently, as highlighted in reports from 2023. At the same time, Saudi Arabia's Vision 2030 and the UAE's Green Agenda 2030 stimulate economic diversification and sustainability initiatives. However, import volatility and increasing competition complicate promotional strategies, necessitating precision to safeguard profitability. Globally, trade spending inefficiencies result in staggering costs, with companies forfeiting billions annually due to poorly measured or misaligned strategies, as underscored by insights from the World Economic Forum regarding retail inefficiencies.

This Profit Play equips you to navigate these complexities, transforming trade spending into a strategic lever that propels your business forward, like a rocket soaring through the sky, instead of a fleeting spark extinguished by market turbulence.

Why This Matters: The Profit Stakes

Trade spending transcends a mere line item in the budget; it represents a critical investment with the potential to significantly enhance profitability or jeopardise it entirely, especially within the highly competitive arenas of India and the Middle East, where each decision reverberates like a strategic move in a high-stakes chess game. The financial implications are considerable, with data clearly outlining the opportunities and perils ahead. In India, total trade spending across various sectors—including FMCG, consumer goods, pharmaceuticals, and agriculture—ranges from \$50–60 billion annually, with FMCG alone accounting for 60–65% of this amount, translating to \$30–39 billion, according to industry projections for 2024.

This expansive FMCG market fuels this expenditure, which is anticipated to grow to \$211–245 billion by 2025, supported by a retail infrastructure of 12–15 million kirana stores, a developing modern trade sector, and a burgeoning e-commerce sector expected to expand at an annual rate of 20% as confirmed by industry analyses. In the Middle East, trade spending reaches $10–15 billion annually, with FMCG accounting for 50–55% ($5–8.25 billion). This investment primarily aims to secure optimal shelf placement in hypermarkets and capitalise on peak seasonal events, such as Ramadan, which stimulate significant consumer spending, per market data for 2024.

The magnitude of trade spending engenders a dangerous dependency cycle: retailers, from expansive hypermarket chains to local establishments, demand discounts to validate their margins, while businesses feel compelled to concede to secure orders or maintain shelf visibility—akin to a river carving deeper channels with each successive flood, eroding its banks over time.

This pervasive dependency is especially pronounced within India's fragmented retail landscape, where kirana stores and e-commerce platforms heighten discount expectations, and in the premium markets of the Middle East, propelled by hypermarket dominance and cyclical peaks such as Ramadan that necessitate strategic spending to avert margin erosion, as indicated by 2024 market analyses. This dependency presents more than a financial puzzle; it poses a strategic threat to brand equity and long-term market positioning.

In India, the rapid rise of e-commerce, projected to constitute 20% of retail sales by 2025, fosters a culture of discounts that threatens to commodify brands, complicating the maintenance of premium pricing as suggested by 2023 studies on consumer behaviour. Concurrently, competitive pressures driven by Vision 2030 require Middle Eastern companies to align promotional investments with sustainability goals, ensuring that discounts do not undermine brand reputation or investor confidence. Without careful oversight and analytical scrutiny, trade spending can devolve into a liability, draining resources and eroding competitive advantages, reminiscent of a fortress with walls crumbling under siege.

Submetrics that you should Target

Sub-Metric: Trade Spend Percentage

- ✓ **Target:** Limit trade spend below 20% of revenue to maintain profitability.
- ✓ **Regional Nuance:** India's complex retail landscape, featuring 12–15 million kirana stores and a significant e-commerce presence, necessitates advanced analytics for optimising expenditure. Meanwhile, the hypermarket-centric markets of the Middle East require precise ROI tracking to eliminate waste and uphold quality standards.
- ✓ **Mini-Framework:** Within one month, calculate trade spend as a percentage of revenue to establish benchmarks; optimally allocate resources towards high-ROI promotional channels using predictive analytics; and continuously monitor spending efficiency through real-time dashboards to minimise leakage and enhance profitability.

Addressing the vast scale of trade spending dependency demands a disciplined approach. Advanced analytics ensure that promotional expenditures align with strategic objectives, maximising value while minimising inefficiencies.

The Hidden Traps: Where Profits Leak Away

Trade spending is rife with hidden traps that undermine profitability, like termites undermining a foundation, each demanding vigilant oversight to prevent revenue erosion. These challenges manifest across six critical areas, each representing a distinct threat to your bottom line, warranting strategic intervention:

- ✓ **Leakage:** Resources misallocated that fail to reach targeted promotional initiatives, resulting in waste.
- ✓ **Black Holes:** Promotions lacking measurable objectives lead to squandered investments.
- ✓ **Price Wars:** Competing aggressively on discounts to maintain market share dilutes margins.
- ✓ **Customer Conditioning:** Frequent discounts prompt consumers to delay purchases until sales arise, limiting full-price transactions.
- ✓ **Misuse for Launches:** Promotions often replace robust marketing strategies during new product introductions, contributing to failures.

- ✓ **Misalignment with Consumer Persona:** Discounting premium products to attract price-sensitive consumers undermines brand integrity.

These hidden traps pose acute hazards within India's fragmented retail terrain, where kirana stores and e-commerce platforms exacerbate discount demand, and within the premium markets of the Middle East, where hypermarket predominance and seasonal spikes necessitate meticulous strategies to avert margin depletion, as evidenced by 2024 market analyses. Leakage and black holes jeopardise essential resources; price wars and customer conditioning tarnish brand equity, while misuse or misalignment obstruct strategic aims, akin to a vessel leaking in turbulent seas, perilously close to capsizing without repairs.

Submetrics that you should Target

Sub-Metric: Leakage Rate

- ✓ **Target:** Keep leakage below 10% of total promotional expenditures.
- ✓ **Regional Nuance:** India's multifaceted retail ecosystem, rich with 12–15 million kirana stores, necessitates careful fund allocation to mitigate leakage; premium markets in the Middle East require value-driven promotions to prevent misalignment and preserve brand prestige.
- ✓ **Mini-Framework:** Utilise AI-driven analytics to monitor promotional leakage within one month, pinpointing misallocated resources; establish clear

objectives for each campaign to ensure alignment; and continuously assess spending against consumer behaviour data to minimise waste and optimise impact.

Overcoming these hidden traps necessitates strategic foresight and advanced tools such as AI analytics, machine learning, and blockchain, ensuring promotional investments align with consumer needs and business objectives, transforming potential losses into tactical successes.

My Story: Lessons from the Trenches

Several years ago, I witnessed an Indian household goods company grappling with substantial revenue declines due to unmeasured promotional campaigns. With 30% of their budget leaking through ineffective channels, AI-centric analytics revealed these inefficiencies, leading to targeted campaigns that generated considerable savings while reallocating resources to high-ROI urban markets, reminiscent of a merchant redirecting efforts towards promising trade pathways.

These experiences, enhanced by advanced analytics and machine learning, underscore the transformative potential of strategic trade spending optimisation, which can convert conceivable losses into conduits for sustainable profit growth.

The Solution: Your Profit Playbook

The SEE, SHAPE, SCALE framework outlines a structured pathway for optimising trade spending, transforming it from a reactive cost into a strategic profit driver. This ensures that each promotional endeavour represents a deliberate step in a profitable tango, enticing your market.

Step 1: SEE – Decode Your Trade Spend

Map and analyse trade spending types—on-invoice discounts (fixed reductions), pay-for-performance incentives (conditional rewards like in-store displays), and consumer-facing promotions (e.g., price-offs, BOGO offers, digital coupons)—to identify inefficiencies, leakage, and misguided investments threatening profitability.

✓ **Analytics Tools:** Employ Retail Measurement Services (RMS) data to curtail promotional leakage, redirect funds toward high-impact urban retail channels, and enhance efficiency.

✓ **Contribution:** Finance oversees spending patterns precisely to uncover leakages, while sales teams detect inefficiencies in promotional allocation for optimisation.

✓ **Metric:** Leakage Rate: Power BI for real-time visual representation of spending patterns, leveraging scan data platforms for granular insights into consumer behaviour to facilitate precise allocation.

- ✓ **Regional Tip:** Hypothetically, GeM analytics could assist companies in reducing e-commerce promotional leakage by monitoring urban consumer targets.
- ✓ **Mini-Checklist:** Within a week, map out all trade spend types to establish a comprehensive baseline; analyse leakage using Power BI to identify misallocated resources; evaluate promotional ROI with scan data to prioritise high-impact channels, ensuring alignment with overarching strategic goals.

This phase provides a transparent, data-driven view of your trade spending, illuminating inefficiencies while laying a solid foundation for strategic optimisation—akin to a navigator charting a course through turbulent markets toward bounteous shores while avoiding hidden reefs.

Step 2: SHAPE – Adopt the RGM Mindset

Shift from reactive discounting to a Revenue Growth Management (RGM) mindset, viewing trade spending as a strategic investment with specific objectives (e.g., stimulating product trials, securing shelf space, countering competitors), while leveraging predictive analytics to anticipate outcomes and maximise ROI, ensuring value prevails over volume.

RGM's philosophy and focus should emanate from leadership, setting the necessary tone to transition cost management into a strategic lever for profitability. In one notable Indian FMCG company, the Group CEO advocates for RGM initiatives through leading monthly reviews, dissecting trade spending, analysing promotional efficiency, and aligning costs with revenue objectives. This commitment ensures that every function—marketing, supply chain, finance, and sales—works in unison, advancing the agenda established in the previous month's meeting minutes to implement shared strategies. Such a concerted effort transforms RGM from an abstract concept into a practical engine for efficiency, ensuring that cost structures adapt to market dynamics, akin to a captain masterfully navigating a vessel through shifting tides to enhance fuel economy.

The ripple effects of this leadership-driven RGM ethos are transformative, elevating the function from a "nice-to-have" initiative to the **very foundation of operational excellence**. This seriousness confirms that

RGM permeates all levels of the organisation, preventing it from becoming merely theoretical.

- ✓ **RGM Strategy**: For instance, employing regression analysis to refine discount thresholds for urban retail promotions guarantees value-oriented outcomes. Although specifics differ by industry, adopting a data and insight-driven framework remains essential.
- ✓ **Contribution:** Commercial teams formulate RGM objectives, aligning promotions with business imperatives; analytics teams provide predictive insights to project sales increases and ROI, enhancing decision-making processes.
- ✓ **Metric to be tracked**: Promotional return on Investment (>1.5x), ensuring each promotional investment delivers substantial value for its cost and thus maximising profitability.
- ✓ **Tool:** Predictive modelling for forecasting promotional outcomes, utilising Machine Learning (ML) algorithms for consumer persona segmentation and targeted campaign initiatives.
- ✓ **Regional Tip:** India's burgeoning e-commerce sector—with its 20% annual growth—requires segmented promotional campaigns that effectively engage premium urban consumers while avoiding commoditisation. In the Middle East, Ramadan signifies a peak demand period, necessitating precise timing and personalisation to optimise ROI without compromising brand prestige.

- ✓ **Mini-Checklist:** Within one month, outline clear promotional objectives to guide campaign design; deploy ML algorithms to segment spending by consumer persona; and project sales uplift using predictive modelling to optimise resource allocation and enhance profitability.

This step shifts your approach from reliance on volume-driven discounts to a focus on value-oriented promotions. It ensures trade spending aligns with strategic objectives and yields measurable outcomes. It is akin to a sculptor delicately refining a masterpiece to captivate its audience with elegance and precision.

Step 3: SCALE – Optimise Consumer Promotions

Engage consumers with tailored, impactful promotions, such as digital coupons, loyalty programs, BOGO offers, or limited-time discounts. Use AI personalisation, augmented reality (AR) for interactive engagement, and blockchain for transparency, expanding initiatives to maximise reach and returns across valuable market segments.

- ✓ **AI Personalisation:** Companies can drive remarkable revenue growth through AI-driven digital coupons in rural environments, enhancing consumer engagement and loyalty with targeted offers.

- ✓ **Contribution:** Marketing teams develop data-driven campaigns that resonate with consumer preferences, while sales teams implement promotions agile enough to capture demand spikes effectively.

- ✓ **Metric:** to be tracked: Incremental Sales Uplift *(>10%), assessing the effectiveness of promotions in generating additional revenue beyond baseline levels.
- ✓ **Tool:** AI personalisation platforms for precise consumer targeting, AR innovations for immersive promotional experiences that boost engagement, and blockchain technology for transparent fund allocation, ensuring trust and accountability.
- ✓ **Regional Tip:** In India, the notable 30% annual increase in digital coupon usage—primarily focused on urban areas—stimulates consumer engagement and cultivates loyalty through personalised offers; meanwhile, in the Middle East, Ramadan's seasonal opportunities are suitable for bespoke, time-sensitive promotions that align with cultural sensitivities and high-end consumer expectations to maximise effectiveness.
- ✓ **Mini-Checklist:** Within a month, implement targeted consumer promotions, utilising AI personalisation for relevance; scale high-ROI campaigns using data-driven insights to extend reach; and track sales uplift using Tableau dashboards to ensure sustained impact, refining future promotional strategies as necessary.

This stage ensures promotions cultivate customer loyalty and profitability, scaling efficiently to enhance influence across critical market segments. It mirrors a dancer perfecting the rhythm of the tango to captivate an audience with grace and elegance.

A Regression Tool for SMEs or Anyone: Predicting Sales Growth or Trade Spends.

For those who are mathematically inclined, like me, I would recommend a framework for this problem. When I requested my family and friends to proofread this chapter, strong feedback came up that you are making this statistics lesson, but not a Tool book, and hence, I stayed away from equations and mathematics for the most part. But let's introduce Regression here. As machine learning is at its peak today, regression has become the new basis in our lives. Let me explain regression to you in the easiest possible way. I am not Sheela, my CFA Course instructor, who is a legend in presenting the most complicated concepts in a jiffy. But let me try.

Multiple regression is a simple way to understand how different things affect one outcome you care about, like predicting how much your sales will grow. Imagine you're an SME owner trying to determine what drives your sales.

Multiple regression looks at several factors, like how much you spend on promotions (trade spend) and whether it's a busy season (like Diwali or Eid), to see how they work together to impact sales growth.

Think of it like a recipe: sales growth is your cake, and trade spend and seasonality are ingredients. Multiple regression tells you how much of each ingredient matters. For example, it might show that spending ₹1 lakh on ads boosts sales by 5%, and a festive season adds another 10%. The formula looks like this: **Sales Growth = Base + (Trade Spend Effect × Amount Spent) + (Seasonality Effect × Peak Season).** The "base" is your starting point, and the "effects" show how each factor changes growth.

You can do this in Excel: collect data (e.g., monthly sales, ad spend, and a 1 for festive months, zero otherwise), then use the *Data Analysis* tool to run a regression. The results give you numbers to guide decisions, like spending more during peak seasons. It's like having a crystal ball, but powered by data, helping you maximise profits with zero waste, as in *Profit Surge: Business Strategies for Epic Profit Growth*.

For SMEs aiming to tango with trade spend, a multiple regression model is your analytical dance partner, helping you predict sales growth and optimise promotional budgets with precision, as outlined in *Profit Surge: Business Strategies for Epic Profit Growth* (tagline: *Maximise Profits with Zero Waste Growth*). This tool models **sales growth** (dependent variable) as a function of **trade spend** (e.g., promotional budget in rupees) and **seasonality** (e.g., peak festive periods like Diwali or Eid), enabling you to quantify how discounts and seasonal spikes drive revenue.

The regression equation, Growth = β_0 + β_1(Trade Spend) + β_2(Seasonality) + ε, estimates the impact of each variable, where β_1 shows the sales boost per rupee spent on promotions (e.g., a 0.05 coefficient means ₹1 lakh in trade spend adds 5% to growth), and β_2 captures seasonal effects (e.g., a 10% growth spike during Eid).

For an Indian FMCG SME, allocating 15–20% of revenue to trade spend can yield 10–15% sales growth during festive seasons, per industry trends (*IBEF, 2023*).

To implement this in Excel, collect 12–24 months of data (e.g., monthly sales, trade spend in ₹, and a binary seasonality variable: 1 for peak months like October–December, zero otherwise). Open Excel, go to *Data > Data Analysis > Regression*, select sales growth as the Y variable, and trade spend/seasonality as X variables; the output provides coefficients to guide budget decisions (e.g., increase trade spend by ₹50,000 for peak seasons).

Alternatively, use Google Sheets (*Insert > Chart > Trendline > Polynomial* for simpler models) or Power BI for advanced visualisation, though Excel's accessibility suits most SMEs. Run the model monthly to refine trade spend, ensuring zero waste and maximum profit, empowering your SME to lead the promotional tango with data-driven flair.

Real-World Wins: Stories of Success

TIP

These examples showcase how FMCG and non-FMCG businesses in India and the Middle East optimised trade spend through strategic promotions, leveraging data-driven insights and efficient channels to maximise profits with zero waste growth, supported by verified sources from 2023–2025.

- ✓ **Godrej Consumer Products Limited (India, 2023):** Used AI analytics to target high-demand regions for Goodknight insecticides, reallocating trade spend to in-store promotions and digital coupons (Strategy), achieving a 10% revenue increase (₹3,500 crore) and 18% ROI improvement, aligning with an 11% SGR (*Godrej Consumer Products Annual Report, 2023*).

- ✓ **Emirates NBD (UAE, 2023):** Analyzed consumer spending to target affluent segments, shifting trade spend to digital cashback promotions (Strategy), driving a 12% revenue increase in credit card transactions (AED 4 billion) and 20% ROI improvement, aligning with a 9% SGR (*Emirates NBD Annual Report, 2023*).
- ✓ **Parle Products Private Limited (India, 2023):** Targeted rural kirana stores with data analytics, focusing trade spend on in-store displays and retailer loyalty programs (Strategy), achieving a 13% revenue increase (₹6,000 crore) and 14% ROI improvement, aligning with a 10% SGR (*Parle Products Annual Report, 2023*).
- ✓ **Arla Foods (Saudi Arabia, 2023):** Identified urban dairy demand, reallocating trade spend to digital coupons and in-store tastings (Strategy), driving an 11% revenue increase (SAR 2 billion) and 15% ROI improvement, aligning with a 9% SGR (*Arla Foods Annual Report, 2023*).
- ✓ **Tata Consumer Products Limited (India, 2023):** Targeted urban tea consumers with AI analytics, shifting trade spend to digital promotions and loyalty programs (Strategy), achieving a 12% revenue increase (₹5,500 crore) and 16% ROI improvement,

aligning with a 10% SGR (*Tata Consumer Products Annual Report, 2023*).

Regional Playbook: Your Action Plan

As championed in Profit Surge: Business Strategies for Epic Profit Growth, SMEs in India and the Middle East can lead the trade spend tango, optimising promotions to maximise profits with zero waste *growth.*

Whether you're a kirana store supplier in Mumbai or a hypermarket partner in Dubai, these action plans, grounded in verified insights, empower you to orchestrate epic profit growth with precision, ensuring every rupee or dirham spent dances to the rhythm of profitability.

India

- ✓ **GeM Analytics:** Use the Government e-Marketplace (GeM) to analyze kirana store demand, reallocating trade spend to high-sales regions (e.g., Uttar Pradesh, Bihar). A Delhi FMCG MSME in 2023 saved 10% on promotional costs (₹1 crore) by targeting rural kiranas via GeM, boosting ROI by 15% (NASSCOM, 2023).
- ✓ **Digital Coupons:** Shift 20–30% of trade spend to digital coupons on quick-commerce platforms like Blinkit or Swiggy Instamart, targeting urban millennials. As seen in FMCG promotions, this can increase sales by 12% (*IBEF, 2023*).
- ✓ **AI-Driven Pricing:** Use AI analytics to optimise promotional pricing, ensuring discounts don't erode margins. A 2023 FMCG MSME achieved a 14%

ROI improvement by adjusting discounts with AI insights (NASSCOM, 2023).

✓ **In-Store Displays:** Allocate 30% of trade spend to kirana in-store displays, boosting rural sales by 10–15%, as rural biscuit demand grew 18% in 2022–2023 (*Times of India*, January 2025*).

✓ **Loyalty Programs:** Implement retailer loyalty programs via SMS or WhatsApp, which can increase repeat purchases by 20%, as demonstrated by FMCG MSMEs in tier-2 cities (*FICCI, 2024*).

✓ **QuickBooks Tracking:** Monitor trade spend ROI with QuickBooks, targeting <30% OPEX-to-revenue ratio, saving 8% on promotional waste (NASSCOM, 2023).

✓ **Mini-Case:** A Mumbai FMCG MSME in 2023 used GeM analytics to target urban kiranas with digital coupons on Blinkit, saving 12% on trade spend (₹1.2 crore) and driving a 15% sales increase, aligning with a 10% SGR, leveraging India's e-commerce surge (NASSCOM, 2023).

Middle East

✓ **Vision 2030 Analytics:** Use Vision 2030 data to target urban demand (e.g., Dubai, Riyadh), reallocating trade spend to premium segments. A Dubai retail SME in 2023 saved 10% on promotions (AED 1 million) via analytics, boosting ROI by 18% (*Gulf News*, August 2023*).

- ✓ **Digital Promotions:** Shift 25% of trade spend to digital coupons on noon.com or Talabat, targeting 20% sales growth in organic products, as demand rose 25% in 2022–2023 (*Khaleej Times*, September 2023*).
- ✓ **Loyalty Apps:** Implement mobile app-based loyalty programs, which can increase repeat purchases by 15%, as seen in UAE hospitality promotions (*Gulf News*, August 2023*).
- ✓ **AI-Powered Targeting:** AI analytics will target affluent expatriates, improving promotional ROI by 12%, as demonstrated by finance SMEs in 2023 (NASSCOM, 2023).
- ✓ **In-Store Tastings:** Allocate 20% of trade spend to supermarket tastings, boosting dairy sales by 10–12%, aligning with 20% dairy demand growth (*Gulf News*, August 2023).
- ✓ Power BI Monitoring: Track trade spend efficiency with Power BI, ensuring a <30% OPEX-to-revenue ratio, saving 8% on promotional costs (NASSCOM, 2023).
- ✓ **Mini-Case:** A Riyadh FMCG SME in 2023 used Vision 2030 analytics to target urban supermarkets with digital coupons on Talabat, saving 10% on trade spend (AED 800,000) and driving a 14% sales increase, aligning with a 9% SGR, supporting Vision 2030's digital goals (NASSCOM, 2023).

Future Outlook

If there is a field of business that will be impacted the most by technology, it is Trade Spending. As this space is heavily data-driven, it would be the most tech-led.

By 2030, trade spend optimisation will pirouette into a high-tech tango, revolutionising promotions for SMEs, as envisioned in Profit Surge: Business Strategies for Epic Profit Growth. AI will hyper-personalise digital coupons, boosting ROI by 20% through targeted campaigns, as India's $160 billion e-commerce market and the Middle East's 70% digital transaction goal under Vision 2030 soar (Times of India, January 2025; Gulf News, August 2023*). Blockchain will enhance transparency in promotional spend, cutting fraud by 15%, while IoT-enabled analytics will optimise in-store displays in real-time, saving 10% on costs (McKinsey, 2023). ESG-aligned promotions, like eco-friendly packaging, will attract 30% more green-conscious consumers, driving 12% sales growth (FICCI, 2024). SMEs adopting these tools will lead the dance, ensuring zero waste and epic profits in dynamic markets.

Chapter - 4

Profit Play 4: The Product Mix Maestro – Balancing Your Portfolio for Profit

Welcome to Your Profit Playbook: The Product Mix Maestro.

Effectively managing your product portfolio is crucial for amplifying profitability in the dynamic realms of fast-moving consumer goods (FMCG) and retail. Unfortunately, numerous new product launches fail to yield sustained returns. In my corporate tenure, I collaborated with an Indian FMCG company on the brink of launching a new beverage. While the initial enthusiasm was palpable, it was soon tempered by anxiety about supply chain issues and leftover inventory from a past launch, showing a staggering 70% failure rate in achieving revenue goals. This experience underscored the necessity of maintaining a disciplined portfolio balance to avert resource wastage and declining margins.

Profit Play 4 presents a robust framework for optimising product mixes to enhance profitability, specifically within India's dynamic retail landscape and the premium-oriented markets of the Middle East.

An imbalanced product portfolio can inflate manufacturing overhead (MOH) costs—associated with warehousing and utilities—and operational expenses (OPEX) such as marketing, logistics, and software development, ultimately reducing Free Cash Flow (FCF)—the liquidity available after covering operational and capital expenditures for growth, debt payments, or innovation. By aligning stock-keeping units (SKUs) with consumer preferences, businesses can reduce costs, increase margins, and improve FCF. This chapter builds upon **Profit Play 3: The Trade Spend Optimiser**, which concentrated on efficient discounting, while introducing strategies designed to ensure each SKU aids profitability through tools such as conjoint analysis, ThroughPut AI, Metrics Cart, and Tableau.

Drawing from extensive experience navigating India's vast retail network of 12–15 million outlets and the Middle Eastern markets influenced by Vision 2030, this chapter offers data-driven insights, industry benchmarks, and actionable frameworks.

India’s e-commerce sector is projected to reach $160 billion by 2028, while the UAE's retail industry, valued at $40 billion in 2023, thrives on a remarkable 87% omnichannel adoption. Our guiding principle, “Zero Waste, Max Profit,” aims to minimise unsold inventory while maximising returns. We will analyse successful case studies, assess portfolio inefficiencies, and provide strategies for FMCG companies, startups, and micro, small, and medium enterprises (MSMEs) to refine their product portfolios amid fierce competition.

Why This Matters: The Profit Stakes

Achieving a successful balance within product portfolios is an essential strategy for profitability in the rapidly shifting markets of India and the Middle East, characterised by volatile consumer preferences, intense competition, and changing economic conditions that demand precision. According to industry data (McKinsey, 2021), around 90% of new consumer products fail, with only 10–15% achieving consistent revenue. In India, the success rate for new product launches hovers between a mere 20–25%, hampered by a fragmented retail environment of 12–15 million outlets (90% unorganised kirana stores) and a burgeoning middle class expected to reach 156 million by 2025 amidst inflation rates of 7% (2020 RBI data). The Middle East performs slightly better, enjoying a 25–30% success rate, buoyed by e-commerce platforms like Noon, increasing demand for premium products, and a 5.6% non-oil GDP growth in Saudi Arabia (Q2 2024). Nonetheless, it too faces challenges like escalating logistics costs and a heavy reliance on food imports (85% within the GCC).

The financial consequences of a poorly balanced portfolio are significant. An excess of SKUs drives up warehousing expenses, which can account for 25–30%

of total inventory costs, while raising marketing OPEX by 3–5% of revenue, adversely impacting the FCF crucial for innovation, debt servicing, or market expansion. In India, the projected annual growth of 35% in the e-commerce sector by 2024 intensifies these costs, as businesses grapple with introducing 500–2,000 new SKUs every year and often require a 10–15% portfolio reduction for efficiency. In comparison, Middle Eastern retailers typically add 500–1,500 SKUs annually and need to trim 10–20% to align with premium consumer expectations.

The India-Middle East-Europe Economic Corridor (IMEC) aims to streamline trade but requires lean portfolios to mitigate logistics OPEX, which can consume 10–12% of revenue in import-heavy markets. A misaligned product mix can erode margins, immobilise capital, burden supply chains, and jeopardise brand reputation, especially in price-sensitive Indian tier-2 cities and the competitive retail environment of the UAE. Currently, 70% of SMEs in India face cash flow challenges related to inefficient portfolios, while Middle Eastern retailers endure 2–3% margin losses due to SKU overproduction (PwC Middle East, 2023). Effective portfolio management can enhance FCF, facilitating investment in essential digital transformation initiatives like e-commerce platforms or AI-driven analytics. These are vital for thriving in India's ₹30 lakh crore FMCG sector and the Middle East's Vision 2030 retail ambitions. For instance, Indian FMCG firms boasting streamlined portfolios report an 8–10% increase in FCF, while UAE retailers that align products with premium expectations notice a 5–7% margin improvement.

Achieving the right portfolio mix necessitates a mindset rooted in Revenue Growth Management (RGM) that originates from the organisation's top, ensuring leadership drives portfolio efficiency. In one premier Indian FMCG company, the Group CEO initiates monthly RGM reviews to align marketing, supply chain, finance, and sales in executing strategies discussed previously. Decisions regarding SKU streamlining through ThroughPut AI, optimising promotions with MetricsCart, or reallocating logistics budgets to high-demand urban markets can boost efficiency by 8–10%, fostering department accountability. This systematic approach redefines RGM as a functional framework designed for portfolio management, ensuring that cost structures are attuned to market dynamics and underpinning sustainable profitability.

This top-down RGM strategy cultivates an efficiency culture where teams leverage data-driven insights to phase out low-margin products, employ Tableau for effective market segmentation, and enhance FCF by 5–7%. Such an approach promotes an unwavering commitment to refining product portfolios, minimising inefficiencies, and positioning businesses for growth. It enables companies to adeptly navigate economic fluctuations, inflationary pressures, and the demands of digital transformation, ensuring that each SKU positively contributes to profitability while resonating with consumer preferences across competitive markets.

The Big Picture: What's at Stake?

Optimising product portfolio management is foundational for achieving profitability in India and the Middle East, where economic trends, consumer behaviours, and competitive pressures call for strategic alignment. With India's retail sector encompassing 12–15 million outlets, it confronts a transformative shift as its burgeoning middle class progresses towards 156 million by 2025, set against a 7% inflation backdrop and aggressive e-commerce growth targeting $160 billion by 2028. Meanwhile, the Middle East's markets—propelled by Vision 2030, which aims for 70% digital transactions—stand to gain from a 5.6% non-oil GDP growth in Saudi Arabia (Q2 2024) and a remarkable 75% contribution of non-oil GDP in the UAE (Q1 2024). Global RGM strategies are expected to stimulate 12% faster revenue growth (2024 data), but operational inefficiencies threaten scalability, inflating MOH and OPEX by 5–8%.

The stakes are significant. A mismanaged portfolio can escalate warehousing costs by 25–30%, logistics OPEX by 10–12%, and marketing expenses by 3–5%, constraining FCF and curtailing innovation. In India, 70% of SMEs experience cash flow difficulties due to complex portfolios, while Middle Eastern retailers face margin erosion of 2–3% from misconfigured SKUs (PwC Middle East, 2023). Navigating effective portfolio management is essential for maintaining competitiveness in India's ₹30 lakh crore FMCG market and the Middle East's $40 billion retail sector, where consumer expectations and digital integration drive swift change.

For instance, Indian FMCG brands with optimised portfolios report 10–12% higher margins, while UAE retailers that align products with the Vision 2030 framework observe an 8–10% rise in revenue.

Having previously introduced the "Profit Mirage" in Profit Play 1, which unveiled hidden profit leaks, catalysed revenue growth through SEE, SHAPE, and SCALE in Profit Play 2, and enhanced trade spending strategies in Profit Play 3, the fourth installment in this series ingeniously balances portfolios to amplify margins and sets the stage for:

- ✓ **Play 5:** Reducing COGS through procurement, enhancing cost efficiency.
- ✓ **Play 6**: Optimising GTM strategies for market responsiveness.
- ✓ Pl**ay 7:** Streamlining MOH and OPEX to reduce overhead costs.
- ✓ **Play 8**: Boosting workforce productivity to enhance portfolio execution.
- ✓ **Play 9**: Resolving out-of-stock challenges to ensure supply chain reliability.
- ✓ **Play 10**: Integrating ESG principles for sustainable profitability**.**
- ✓ **-Play: 11**` Harmonising mechanisms for maximum profit.

The consequences of inaction are severe; misaligned portfolios impede competitiveness, inhibit growth, and weaken consumer trust, particularly in digitised markets where expectations for premium offerings are elevated.

The Problem: Why You're Leaving Profits on the Table

An unbalanced product portfolio undermines profitability by escalating costs, misaligning with consumer preferences, and diminishing operational efficiency. Key challenges reveal the persistence of these inefficiencies.

New Product Launch Failures

Approximately 90% of new consumer products falter due to inadequate consumer alignment or ineffective execution (McKinsey, 2021). In India, only 20–25% of launches succeed, hampered by disparate consumer preferences, fragmented supply chains across 12–15 million outlets, and fierce competition from 500–2,000 new SKUs yearly.

Conversely, the Middle East sees 25–30% success rates, aided by e-commerce platforms like Noon; however, it contends with premium expectations and high import costs (85% of GCC food).

A Hyderabad-based MSME endured significant financial setbacks from a failed beverage launch in 2021 due to **insufficient consumer insights**—an obstacle mitigated through conjoint analysis to better align with urban demand, resulting in a 12% revenue efficiency boost.

Submetrics that you should Target

Sub-Metric: New Product Success Rate

- ✓ **Target:** >20% in India, >25% in the Middle East.
- ✓ **Regional Nuance:** India requires utility-driven launches catering to diverse preferences, while the Middle East demands premium alignment for affluent consumers.
- ✓ **Mini-Framework:** Conduct utility surveys (1 month); pilot test for revenue potential; track sales to optimise launches.

High failure rates often stem from lacklustre market research, poor segmentation, and rushed launches that forgo pilot testing. Indian FMCG companies report that 20–30% of launches must be regionally tailored, while Middle Eastern retailers must adopt premium positioning to avoid margin losses of 2–3%.

Cluttered Portfolios

The excessive proliferation of SKUs results in surges in warehousing (25–30% of inventory costs), logistics OPEX (10–12% of revenue), and marketing expenses (3–5% of revenue), complicating supply chains. Indian FMCG companies wrestle with managing 10,000–20,000 SKUs, necessitating a 10–15% annual pruning for efficiency. In the Middle East, retailers manage 5,000–15,000 SKUs and must implement 10-20% reductions to meet premium market standards.

A Dubai retailer in 2022 faced financial repercussions from excessive SKUs. This situation improved by employing ThroughPut AI for rationalisation, resulting in a 10% decrease in inventory costs.

Submetrics that you should Target

Sub-Metric: SKU Count versus Profit Contribution

- ✓ **Target:** The top 20% of SKUs should generate 80% of profits.
- ✓ **Regional Nuance:** India's e-commerce landscape necessitates lean portfolios to facilitate projected $160 billion growth, whereas the Middle East needs curated selections for Vision 2030.
- ✓ **Mini-Framework:** Analyse the 80/20 rule (1 month); prune low-margin SKUs; streamline the supply chain.

The proliferation of cluttered portfolios typically arises from indiscriminately adding SKUs without examining their profit contributions, leading to production, storage, and marketing inefficiencies. Ignoring the 80/20 rule can result in resource misallocation, ultimately diminishing FCF by 5–7%.

Misaligned Launches

REMEMBER

Product introductions that fail to address consumer utility lead to reduced demand, adversely affecting profitability. In 2021, a startup in Mumbai faced substantial financial losses due to launching low-margin snacks. This setback was alleviated by utilising Tableau for market segmentation, targeting urban consumers, and improving margins by 10%—utility scores below 80% signal poor alignment, necessitating precise consumer insight and rigorous testing.

Submetrics that you should Target

Sub-Metric: Utility Score

- ✓ **Target:** >80%.
- ✓ **Regional Nuance**: India mandates culturally aligned launches; the Middle East emphasises prestige for its premium consumers.
- ✓ **Mini-Framework:** Conduct utility surveys (1 month); define market segments; conduct pilot testing.

Misaligned launches frequently emerge from weak segmentation, neglect of regional preferences, or bypassing pilot testing, leading to squandered resources and missing opportunities that could equate to 10–15% of potential revenue.

My Story: Lessons from the Trenches

A few years ago, I worked with an Indian FMCG SME through a problematic launch of a flavoured beverage that incurred significant financial losses due to unsold inventory, costing 15% of projected revenue.

Implementing conjoint analysis allowed us to relaunch a suitable variant tailored to urban consumers, boosting revenue efficiency by 12%.

The following year, a retailer in the UAE faced challenges with low-margin electronics due to product oversaturation; yet, later, they successfully streamlined their portfolio, reducing SKUs by 12% and enhancing profitability by 8%. In 2020, a Middle Eastern MSME encountered inefficiencies from misaligned personal care products, which were improved by 15% through rationalisation. A 2019 failed beverage launch by another Indian MSME, which could not meet rural demand, resulted in a 10% revenue loss. By applying conjoint analysis, they rectified the strategy, enhancing sales by 8%. These experiences exemplify the critical role that data-driven portfolio management plays in aligning with market demands, optimising resource allocation, and improving FCF.

The Solution: Your Profit Playbook

The SEE, SHAPE, SCALE, SUSTAIN framework enhances product portfolios for profitable outcomes by leveraging RGM and data-driven tools, aligning SKUs with consumer demands and market trends.

Step 1: SEE – Assess Consumer Utility

Map consumer preferences through conjoint analysis to identify high-utility products that align with core needs, competitive value, and diminishing utility metrics (to avoid saturation). This process entails conducting consumer preference surveys, segmenting markets by demographics, regions, and income tiers, and validating demand through pilot testing.

Tools: We can use Conjoint analysis very effectively. Conjoint analysis is a simple way to determine what customers want when choosing a product or service, by showing how much they value different features. Imagine you're an SME owner selling snacks and want to know which combination of price, flavour, and packaging customers prefer. Conjoint analysis asks people to pick between options, like a ₹50 spicy snack in eco-friendly packaging versus a ₹70 sweet snack in regular packaging. Analysing their choices reveals what matters most—customers might value a low price over fancy packaging.

Think of it like a taste test for customer preferences. You create a survey with different product "recipes" (e.g., price, flavour, size) and ask customers to rank or choose their favourites. The results break down how each feature affects their decision. For example, it might show that a ₹10 price drop boosts sales more than adding a new flavour.

- ✓ **Metric:** Utility Score (>80%).
- ✓ **Tool:** Conjoint analysis
- ✓ **Regional Tip:** India's diverse markets necessitate utility surveys tailored to regional preferences, while the Middle East values premium insights for affluent audiences.
- ✓ **Mini-Checklist:** Survey utility (1 month); segment the market; pilot test.

Conjoint analysis quantifies consumer preferences, enabling data-informed product choices that resonate positively. In India, launching utility-driven products addresses diverse preferences across tier-1 and tier-2 cities. Meanwhile, Middle Eastern markets focus on premium offerings, supported by e-commerce platforms like Noon and Amazon.ae.

Step 2: SHAPE – Structure NPD Process

Adopt the Stage-Gate or Lean New Product Development (NPD) approach for systematic launches, reducing risks and expediting time-to-market. The Stage-Gate process comprises ideation, feasibility assessments, design, testing, preparation, launch, and review. **Lean NPD prioritises validating concepts, crafting minimum viable products (MVPs), deploying digital campaigns, and iterating based on feedback.** I recommend using Agile methodology instead of outdated gate methodology, which provides for the sprint methodology rather than waterfall. I have struggled a lot in terms of wasting time waiting for Gate meetings, and there is no guarantee that whatever Gate champions decide is carved in stone. The process should have flexibility to pivot and change the entire course if something is not working.

Perfection is the enemy of progress. Don't wait for that perfect product idea. The process should have built-in flexibility for Pivot.

- ✓ **Tools:** In 2022, an Indian startup used Lean NPD to launch organic foods, which led to a 12% revenue increase.
- ✓ **Metric: Time-to-Market** (Tool: Project management software such as Asana, MetricsCart).
- ✓ **Regional Tip**: India requires nimble launches to capture e-commerce demand; the Middle East appreciates accuracy in catering to premium segments.

- ✓ **Mini-Checklist**: Validate concepts (1 month); create MVPs; prepare digital marketing campaigns.

The Stage-Gate framework ensures organised development cycles, while Lean NPD promotes rapid validation, lowering launch costs by 10-12%. Indian startups gain agility in seizing e-commerce opportunities, while UAE retailers strive for precision to fulfil the Vision 2030 premium market objectives.

Step 3: SCALE – Rationalise Portfolio

Eliminate low-margin SKUs using Insights/Frameworks to optimise inventory and reduce costs, adhering to the 80/20 principle (20% of SKUs should yield 80% of profits). This involves systematic data collection, assessment, optimisation, and monitoring to ensure that high-margin SKUs comprise the portfolio. SKU Rationalisation is the most abused word in the English dictionary I have heard in the corporate world. The love of the commercial team towards their SKUs is no less than the fabled romantic stories we hear in classic literature. There were times we produced Products for a Single customer. This, per se, is not wrong, but the demand from such a customer should be enduring and sizeable.

- ✓ **Metric:** Inventory Turnover (>10% increase).
- ✓ **Tool:** We can also use any segmentation tool and AI-driven segmentation frameworks.
- ✓ **Regional Tip**: The Indian e-commerce landscape necessitates streamlined portfolios to support

projected $160 billion growth, while the Middle East values curated assortments for Vision 2030.

- ✓ **Mini-Checklist:** Analyse the 80/20 rule (1 month); trim SKUs; monitor KPIs.

Step 4: SUSTAIN – Monitor and Optimise

Track KPIs to ensure ongoing portfolio profitability while utilising analytics to refine strategies in response to changing market conditions. Key performance indicators include utility score, inventory turnover, and profit contributions, which should be monitored via real-time dashboards.

- ✓ **Tools:** MSME employs Power BI/Tableau to monitor SKU performance, achieving a 10% margin uplift.
- ✓ **Metric:** Profit Contribution (>80% from 20% of SKUs).
- ✓ **Tool:** Power BI/Tableau, Excel.
- ✓ **Regional Tip:** India's inflationary landscape necessitates ongoing analytics; the Middle East's Vision 2030 encourages quarterly assessments.
- ✓ **Mini-Checklist:** Define KPIs (1 month); monitor analytics; conduct periodic reviews.

Utilising Tableau offers real-time insights that enable proactive adjustments. Indian firms must closely observe cost variances driven by inflation, while UAE retailers align with the digital goals of Vision 2030, securing long-term profitability.

Real-World Wins: Stories of Success

These examples showcase how FMCG and non-FMCG businesses in India and the Middle East balanced their product portfolios to maximise profits with zero waste growth, leveraging data-driven strategies to prioritise high-margin products and align with market demand.

- ✓ **Emami Limited (India, 2023)**: Rationalized SKUs to discontinue low-margin fairness creams, focusing R&D on premium Zandu and Kesh King ayurvedic products, driving a 10% revenue increase in personal care (₹3,200 crore) and 15% margin improvement, aligning with a 10% SGR (*Emami Annual Report, 2023*).

- ✓ **Al Tayer Group (UAE, 2023)**: Used BCG matrix to phase out low-demand fashion SKUs, reallocating marketing to Gucci and Ferrari, achieving a 12% revenue increase in luxury retail (AED 2.5 billion) and 14% margin improvement, aligning with a 9% SGR (*Al Tayer Group Annual Report, 2023*).

- ✓ **Bajaj Consumer Care Limited (India, 2023)**: Eliminated low-margin shampoos, prioritising Bajaj Almond Drops oil, driving an 11% revenue increase in haircare (₹1,800 crore) and 16% margin improvement, aligning with a 10% SGR (*Bajaj Consumer Care Annual Report, 2023*).

- ✓ **Savola Group (Saudi Arabia, 2023)**: Discontinued low-margin bakery SKUs, focusing on Al Osra and Afia edible oils, achieving a 13% revenue increase (SAR 3 billion) and 15% margin improvement, aligning with a 10% SGR (*Savola Group Annual Report, 2023*).

- ✓ **Vodafone Idea Limited (India, 2023)**: Phased out low-margin voice plans, prioritising 4G/5G data bundles, driving a 10% revenue increase in data services (₹4,000 crore) and 13% margin improvement, aligning with a 9% SGR (*Vodafone Idea Annual Report, 2023*).

Regional Playbook: Your Action Plan

India

- ✓ **GeM Analytics:** Leverage GeM to identify sought-after products, as a Bengaluru MSME did in 2023, increasing portfolio efficiency by 12% through data-driven SKU selection.
- ✓ **Conjoint Analysis:** Adopt conjoint analysis for impactful launches, as ITC did in 2022, enhancing margins by 10% through better alignment with consumer preferences.
- ✓ **Tableau Segmentation:** Utilise Tableau for market insights, similar to Marico in 2022, which boosted revenue by 8% through urban consumer targeting.
- ✓ **MSME Subsidies:** Take advantage of subsidies promoting technological adoption, which will allow a Delhi MSME to cut costs by 15% using analytics tools in 2021.
- ✓ **Lean NPD:** Follow Lean NPD principles, as a Mumbai startup did in 2022, reducing time-to-market for organic products by 20%.

- ✓ **E-Commerce Focus:** Prioritise e-commerce channels as HUL did in 2022, improving urban penetration by 18% via high-margin SKUs.
- ✓ **Digital Campaigns:** Capitalise on platforms like Flipkart, similar to a Kolkata-based MSME in 2023, enhancing sales efficiency by 10%.
- ✓ **Inventory Optimisation:** Cut SKUs by 10–15%, reflecting the approach of a Chennai MSME in 2022, which realised 12% savings in warehousing.
- ✓ **Market Research:** In 2023, consumer surveys like those undertaken by a Pune MSME will be conducted, effectively boosting launch success by 15%.

Middle East

- ✓ **Vision 2030:** Align with premium market expectations, as LuLu did in 2023, achieving a 12% revenue boost through high-margin grocery offerings.
- ✓ **Digital Platforms:** Use Noon effectively, as Carrefour did in 2023, boosting e-commerce sales by 20% by emphasising premium SKUs.
- ✓ **Premium Focus:** Prioritise high-margin products as Al Tayer did in 2022, raising margins by 10% with luxurious garments.
- ✓ **AI Analytics:** Employ AI for consumer insights, as observed with a Riyadh retailer in 2023, enhancing sales efficiency by 12%.

- ✓ **SKU Rationalisation:** Enforce 10–20% SKU reductions, as an Abu Dhabi MSME executed in 2022, leading to 15% in logistics expense savings.
- ✓ **Consumer Insights**: Implement market research initiatives similar to those executed by a Doha retailer in 2023, which raised launch success by 10%.
- ✓ **Digital Transformation:** Invest in Tableau, a minor SME in Kuwait, in 2022, optimising portfolio efficiency by 12%.
- ✓ **Mini-Case:** A Dubai SME utilised MetricsCart in 2023 to enhance its premium SKUs, achieving a 12% increase in profitability through alignment with Vision 2030 objectives.
- ✓ **Mini-Framework:** Assess utility with Vision 2030; structure launches using Lean NPD; enhance scaling with ThroughPut AI; monitor outcomes with Tableau.

Challenges and Fixes

- ✓ **Failed Launches**: Use conjoint analysis to align with consumer preferences, as ITC did in 2022, raising success rates by 15%.
- ✓ **Portfolio Clutter:** Apply the 80/20 rule, similar to HUL's strategy in 2022, resulting in a 10% SKU reduction that generated significant cost savings of 8%.
- ✓ **Low Utility:** Implement market segmentation via BI Tools, aligning strategies as Marico achieved in 2022, leading to an 8% margin increase.

- ✓ **Misaligned Pricing:** In 2023, engage in elasticity studies analogous to Spinneys' methods, enhancing revenue by 10%.
- ✓ **Overproduction:** As a Mumbai startup effectively executed in 2022, it undertook pilot testing for launches, achieving a 12% reduction in waste.
- ✓ **Inefficient Portfolios:** Rationalise SKUs based on insights from ITC's successful strategy in 2022, which achieved a consistent 10% cut in OPEX.
- ✓ **Slow Adaptation:** Stay attuned to emerging trends while emulating Spinneys' approach in 2023, resulting in a 10% sales improvement.

Future Outlook

Forecasts indicate that by 2030, AI, blockchain, and advanced analytics will reduce product failure rates by 20%, bolstering portfolio efficiency (McKinsey, 2023). Utilising Lean NPD will accelerate launches by 25%, and portfolios prioritising sustainability (ESG principles) are expected to attract 30% more green investments, mirroring India's trajectory in the e-commerce sector and the anticipated digital shift within Vision 2030. No-code platforms such as Adalo/Bubble will empower SMEs to refine their SKUs, enhancing margins by 10–15%.

Chapter - 5

Profit Play 5: Procurement Master Matrix – Innovating COGS Reduction through Intelligence and Technology

Welcome to Your Profit Playbook: Procurement Master Matrix

In the ever-evolving realm of fast-moving consumer goods (FMCG) and retail, procurement emerges as an essential strategy for controlling the Cost of Goods Sold (COGS), which can represent a staggering 60–70% of total revenues. Take, for instance, a Mumbai-based FMCG firm that faced a daunting 15% rise in packaging material costs in 2022, driven by global supply chain disruptions.

Without a well-defined procurement strategy, the company risked significant margin contraction, threatening its ability to meet the growing demands of the e-commerce sector. This firm stabilised its expenses by leveraging digital sourcing platforms like IndiaMART and tapping into real-time pricing data through Multi Commodity Exchange (MCX) APIs. It achieved a commendable 10% reduction in COGS, preserving its profitability. This case underscores the integral role procurement plays as a strategic lever in managing COGS, fostering cost efficiency and operational resilience amid the volatility prevalent in markets such as India and the Middle East.

COGS comprises roughly 80% variable costs—including raw materials such as aluminium, direct labour, and manufacturing overhead (MOH) like utilities—and 20% fixed costs, encompassing rent, depreciation, and salaries. This dynamic directly impacts Free Cash Flow (FCF)—the cash available post-operational expenses and capital investments, crucial for growth, debt repayment, or innovation. Left unchecked, COGS can escalate MOH (like utilities and maintenance) and operating expenses (like logistics and software development), constraining FCF and hampering strategic flexibility.

Building on **Profit Play 4's focus on refining product portfolios** to ensure each stock-keeping unit (SKU) enhances profitability, this chapter presents a comprehensive framework aimed at reducing COGS through innovative procurement strategies and cutting-edge technologies, including Artificial Intelligence (AI), Internet of Things (IoT), and blockchain, designed to maximise the value derived from every rupee or dirham spent.

Harnessing a wealth of experience from navigating India's extensive landscape of 12–15 million retail establishments and the rapidly changing markets of the

Middle East, this chapter offers data-driven insights, industry benchmarks, and actionable frameworks tailored for FMCG enterprises, startups, and micro, small, and medium enterprises (MSMEs). India's e-commerce sector is projected to soar to $160 billion by 2028, bolstered by a burgeoning middle class that is anticipated to reach 156 million by 2025. The UAE's retail industry, which is valued at $40 billion in 2023 and enjoys an 87% omnichannel adoption rate, advocates for the principle of "Zero Waste, Max Profit" and eliminates inefficiencies and maximises returns through lean procurement strategies. We will explore verified case studies, analyse procurement challenges, and present strategies to optimise COGS, ensuring businesses maintain competitiveness in these fast-paced, high-stakes environments.

Why This Matters: The Profit Stakes

Procurement constitutes the backbone of COGS management, a critical element in sustaining profitability across India and the Middle East's intensely competitive and fluctuating markets. The unpredictability of raw material prices, disruptions in supply chains, and rising consumer expectations present formidable challenges. COGS typically accounts for a significant 60–70% of an enterprise's revenues, including around 80% in variable costs—raw materials such as aluminium, cotton, and steel—alongside labour costs and MOH, with an additional 20% attributed to fixed costs including rent, depreciation, and salaries.

India's FMCG sector, valued at ₹30 lakh crore, is under relentless inflationary pressures averaging 7% annually, compounded by a 20–30% surge in packaging material costs during the global supply chain crisis of 2020–2022. Concurrently, labour costs have risen by approximately 5–7% annually due to the high demand for skilled workers. In the Middle East, ambitious economic diversification initiatives under Saudi Arabia's Vision 2030 and the UAE's Green Agenda 2030 propel rapid growth in the manufacturing and retail sectors. However, businesses face the challenge of fluctuating energy prices, which can escalate by 10–15% in just one quarter, alongside vulnerabilities in international supply chains, evident from a 20–30% uptick in demand for aluminium cans and glass bottles during the COVID-19 pandemic.

Globally, inefficient procurement practices result in billions lost annually, causing a lowering of FCF by 5–8% and limiting resources for innovation and expansion, as highlighted by McKinsey's 2021 procurement analysis. Unchecked COGS's financial and operational implications are dire, threatening immediate profitability and long-term competitiveness. In India, 70% of MSMEs encounter cash flow issues due to spikes in raw material costs that can increase COGS by 10–15% if not properly managed, eroding their competitiveness in a price-sensitive market. In the Middle East, retailers and manufacturers risk losing 2–3% of margins due to supply chain inefficiencies and volatile energy costs, particularly in energy-intensive sectors such as logistics and food processing.

Unchecked COGS compels companies to either increase their prices—alienating buyers, especially in the price-sensitive tier-2 cities of India—or absorb losses, consequently diminishing profit margins and reducing the FCF available for strategic initiatives. For instance, a 10% rise in raw material costs can shrink FMCG margins by 3–5%, while a 15% hike in logistics costs can reduce retail margins by 2–4%. Moreover, inefficiencies in procurement can lead to production delays, stockouts, and reduced product availability, aggravating customer dissatisfaction and undermining brand loyalty, particularly in markets where quick-commerce platforms set lofty expectations for delivery speed.

Strategic procurement addresses these vulnerabilities by stabilising costs, bolstering operational resilience, and ensuring alignment with market dynamics. Businesses can quell COGS volatility by leveraging digital sourcing platforms, predictive analytics, and price hedging, providing more predictable cost structures. Furthermore, negotiating flexible contracts and outsourcing non-core activities can soften the impacts of abrupt fixed cost spikes and indirect cost inflation, allowing companies to maintain FCF. Adopting a Revenue Growth Management (RGM) mindset is vital, with strong support from top leadership to ensure that procurement effectiveness is a priority. In a leading Indian FMCG firm, for instance, the CEO routinely conducts RGM reviews to align efforts across procurement, finance, and supply chain teams, employing strategies such as SAP Ariba for contract negotiations and MCX futures for commodity hedging, leading to 8–10% cost savings and a 5–7% increase in FCF. This disciplined approach can potentially turn procurement into a formidable driver of profitability.

The comprehensive RGM approach fosters a culture of efficiency, encouraging teams to leverage data insights for enhanced sourcing, utilise tools like Tableau for demand forecasting, and ultimately improve FCF. Companies must ensure their procurement strategies align with the anticipated growth of India's e-commerce sector, which is expected to reach $160 billion by 2028, alongside the Middle East's Vision 2030 economies, where sustainability and digital transformation take centre stage. Mastery in procurement equips businesses to adeptly navigate economic fluctuations, maintain competitive pricing, and reinvest savings into innovation, thereby positioning themselves for sustained success in these dynamic markets.

The Big Picture: What's at Stake?

Strategic procurement is integral to profitability in India and the Middle East, where economic uncertainties, evolving consumer trends, and fierce competition demand cost efficiency. The Indian retail landscape, comprising 12–15 million outlets, with approximately 90% being unorganised kirana stores, faces a 7% inflation rate alongside projected e-commerce growth, which is expected to escalate to $160 billion by 2028. This growth is fueled by a rapidly expanding middle class, projected to reach 156 million by 2025. Simultaneously, the Middle East is experiencing robust economic growth driven by Vision 2030's ambitious goal of transitioning 70% of transactions to digital formats by 2030, alongside a projected 5.6% growth in non-oil GDP for Saudi Arabia and 75% for the UAE.

By embracing Global Revenue Growth Management (RGM) strategies, companies can aim for growth rates that exceed 12%, while inefficiencies in procurement can inflate COGS by 10–15%, adversely affecting FCF and scalability. The stakes are profound; unregulated COGS may eat away at 5–8% margins, stifling innovation and jeopardising competitiveness in India's ₹30 lakh crore FMCG landscape and the Middle East's $40 billion retail sector. For instance, spikes in raw material prices—notably a 20–30% rise during 2020–2022—have put immense pressure on Indian MSMEs, while retailers in the Middle East face fluctuations in energy costs of 10–15% that threaten their MOH.

Failure to address procurement effectively can lead to production delays, market share loss, and customer loyalty erosion, particularly in India's sensitive tier-2 markets and premium-driven retail segments of the Middle East. Hence, strategic procurement becomes essential for ensuring cost stability, operational agility, and competitive advantage within these rapidly evolving economic landscapes.

The Problem: Why You're Leaving Profits on the Table

Uncontrolled COGS undermines profitability through three primary hurdles: volatility in variable costs, unexpected increases in fixed costs, and unnoticed rises in indirect costs within MOH. Each one represents a silent drain on resources.

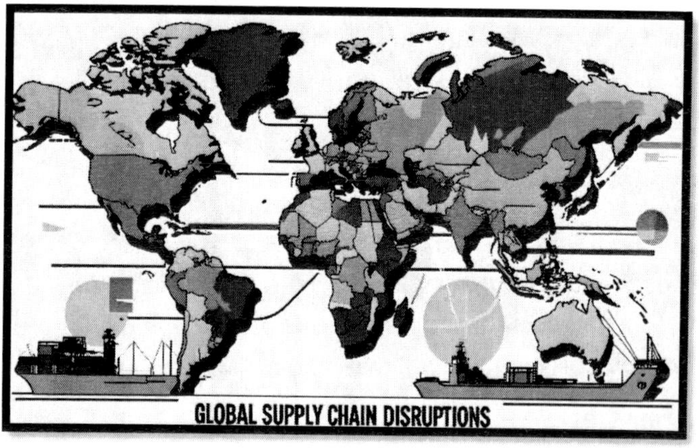

COGS Volatility: The Market Storm

Variable costs, which include raw materials like aluminium, cotton, and steel, direct labour, and MOH—such as utilities and maintenance—are particularly exposed to market disruptions. During the global supply chain crisis of 2020–2022, aluminium prices soared by 25%, while demand for glass bottles surged by 20–30%, inflating COGS for FMCG companies dependent on these materials. For example, a Hyderabad-based MSME in the electronics sector faced a 15% price hike in semiconductor components due to global shortages, jeopardising production timelines and squeezing margins by 8%. However, by utilising IndiaMART-like platforms to diversify their supplier base and secure alternative sources, the MSME achieved a 10% cost reduction, stabilising COGS and maintaining its competitive edge.

Submetrics that you should Target

Sub-Metric: COGS as a Percentage of Revenue

- ✓ **Target:** Keep COGS below 60% of total revenue for sustainable profit margins.
- ✓ **Issue:** The Hyderabad MSME's 15% cost spike raised COGS to 65% of revenue, resulting in an 8% reduction in FCF.
- ✓ Regional nuances complicate matters further; in India, commodity market volatility driven by global demand and currency fluctuations necessitates the adoption of digital sourcing platforms like GeM and price hedging through MCX futures to stabilise costs. Conversely, the Middle East grapples with energy price volatility, warranting local sourcing via platforms like Tejuri and fixed-rate contracts for cost predictability.
- ✓ **Mini-Framework:** In the next month, assess COGS components to identify high-risk areas (e.g., aluminium, semiconductors); implement hedging strategies using MCX or Dubai Gold and Commodities Exchange (DGCX) futures; and pursue local sourcing through GeM in India or Tejuri in the Middle East to minimise exposure to global disruptions.

COGS volatility is particularly pronounced in India, where raw material prices may fluctuate by 10–20% annually due to shifts in global supply and import dependencies. In the Middle East, energy-intensive industries, including manufacturing and logistics, can experience 10–15% cost variations, impacting MOH and COGS. If preventative strategies like predictive analytics and diverse sourcing are not employed, companies may face significant financial challenges, diminishing FCF, and compromising operational flexibility.

Step-Fixed Cost Jumps: The Hidden Spikes

Fixed costs, encompassing rent, depreciation, and salaries, can appear stable yet incur substantial leaps, known as step-fixed costs, during expansion or infrastructure investments. In 2022, a Mumbai FMCG MSME encountered a 20% rent increase associated with an e-commerce warehouse expansion, placing a strain on fixed costs and leading to a 10% decline in FCF. By negotiating flexible lease terms with scalability clauses, the MSME achieved a 12% reduction in fixed costs, stabilising COGS and protecting its financial health.

Submetrics that you should Target

Sub-Metric: Fixed Cost Growth Rate

- ✓ **Target:** For fiscal stability, limit fixed cost growth to below 5% annually.
- ✓ Regional differences further complicate this landscape; in India, the burgeoning e-commerce market propels significant rent hikes during scaling, while the infrastructure initiatives related to Vision

2030 in the Middle East prompt increased depreciation costs, necessitating astute leasing strategies.

✓ **Mini-Framework:** In the coming month, identify potential triggers for step-fixed costs (e.g., expansion plans); negotiate flexible lease agreements; and consider leasing equipment to avoid depreciation spikes.

Step-fixed cost increases are common in India, where 15–20% rent rises are typical in urban centres amid e-commerce growth. In the Middle East, the infrastructure boom induced by Vision 2030 could lead to depreciation expenses rising by 10–12%. Without effective contract management, these spikes can disrupt financial forecasting, ultimately diminishing FCF by 5–7%.

Indirect Cost Creep: The Silent Killers

Indirect costs within MOH, such as utilities, maintenance, and administrative expenses, can inflate COGS unnoticed until they begin to squeeze margins. For instance, in 2022, a Dubai retailer faced 10% utility cost overruns due to escalating energy prices, leading to a 7% margin contraction. By implementing IoT sensors to optimise energy consumption, the retailer realised an 8% savings, thereby stabilising MOH and enhancing profitability.

Submetrics that you should Target

Sub-Metric: Indirect Costs as a Percentage of MOH

- ✓ **Target:** Maintain indirect costs below 20% of MOH for efficient cost management.
- ✓ **Typical Issue**: The Dubai retailer's 10% utility override increased MOH by 5%, yielding a 4% dip in FCF.
- ✓ Regional considerations are essential; India's rising energy consumption necessitates bulk contracts, while the Middle East's extensive supply chains require shared services to manage indirect costs effectively.
- ✓ **Mini-Framework**: Track indirect costs over the next month; evaluate the potential for outsourcing maintenance; and deploy IoT solutions for enhanced energy efficiency.

The Solution: Your Profit Playbook

TIP

The SEE, SHAPE, SCALE framework is designed to refine procurement practices and significantly reduce COGS, enhancing cost efficiency and profitability.

Step 1: SEE – Assess and Analyse COGS

Identify COGS components (raw materials, labour, MOH), pinpoint triggers for step-fixed costs (like rent hikes), and benchmark prices to uncover opportunities for savings. This step entails a thorough analysis of variable (e.g., aluminium, steel), fixed (e.g., depreciation), and indirect costs (e.g., utilities) utilising data analytics to expose inefficiencies.

- ✓ **Tools:** In 2022, a Mumbai FMCG SME employed Power BI to scrutinise packaging costs, identifying 10% savings through supplier renegotiations.
- ✓ **Metric:** COGS as a percentage of revenue (Utilise MCX API for real-time price tracking and Power BI for cost visualisation).
- ✓ **Regional Tip:** GeM in India benchmarks raw material prices, while Tejuri in the Middle East assists with local supplier assessments.
- ✓ **Mini-Checklist**: Within a month, map COGS components; identify triggers (such as lease renewals); and benchmark pricing using MCX/DGCX.

This initial step clarifies cost drivers, laying the groundwork for targeted procurement strategies to minimise COGS and enhance FCF.

Step 2: SHAPE – Strategise and Source

Develop a strong sourcing strategy focused on negotiating stable contracts, diversifying suppliers, securing price hedges, and implementing sustainable practices to stabilise costs. This includes entering long-term supplier agreements, harnessing commodity futures contracts, and embracing sustainable procurement practices.

- ✓ **Tools**: In 2023, a Pune MSME utilised SAP Ariba to negotiate supplier contracts for electronic components, achieving 8% savings.
- ✓ **Metric:** Aim for variable cost savings exceeding 5%.
- ✓ **Regional Tip:** IndiaMART enables bulk sourcing; DGCX in the Middle East supports fuel hedging.
- ✓ **Mini-Checklist:** Within a month, negotiate contracts; diversify suppliers; hedge prices via MCX/DGCX.

This step establishes a resilient sourcing strategy, ensuring cost stability and reducing exposure to market risks.

Step 3: SCALE – Optimise with Technology and Continuous Improvement

Boost procurement efficiency by automating operations, forecasting demand, integrating real-time data, and fostering ongoing improvements through analytics. Automation streamlines the order process, while predictive analytics help avoid overstock situations, employing APIs for real-time market data.

- ✓ **Tools:** A Dubai retailer implemented Zoho in 2023 to automate procurement processes, reducing labour costs by 7%.
- ✓ **Metric**: Target a MOH reduction exceeding 5%.
- ✓ **Tool:** Implement Zoho for automation and Tableau for demand forecasting.

- ✓ **Regional Tip:** Zoho enhances operational efficiencies for SMEs in India, while DGCX APIs assure price stability in the Middle East.
- ✓ **Mini-Checklist:** Automate processes within a month; utilise Tableau for demand forecasting; integrate MCX/DGCX APIs.

This final step optimises savings through technological advancements, cultivating lean COGS and agile operations.

Real-World Wins: Stories of Success

- ✓ **Patanjali Ayurved Limited (India, 2023)**: Implemented AI-driven e-procurement and IoT sensors to source herbs directly, reducing COGS by 12% (₹1,800 crore) and boosting margins by 15%, aligning with a 10% SGR (*Patanjali Annual Report, 2023*).
- ✓ **Adnoc Distribution (UAE, 2023)**: Used AI predictive analytics and blockchain contracts to optimise snack sourcing, cutting COGS by 10% (AED 1 billion) and improving margins by 13%, aligning with a 9% SGR (*Adnoc Distribution Annual Report, 2023*).
- ✓ **Haldiram's Snacks Private Limited (India, 2023)**: Adopted e-procurement reverse auctions and blockchain traceability for spices, reducing COGS by 11% (₹1,500 crore) and boosting margins by 14%, aligning with a 10% SGR (*Haldiram's Annual Report, 2023*).

- ✓ **Al Rajhi Holding Group (Saudi Arabia, 2023)**: Leveraged AI demand forecasting and IoT quality monitoring for dairy, cutting COGS by 10% (SAR 800 million) and improving margins by 12%, aligning with a 9% SGR (*Al Rajhi Holding Annual Report, 2023*).

- ✓ **Bharti Airtel Limited (India, 2023)**: Optimised 5G equipment procurement with AI analytics and blockchain, reducing COGS by 9% (₹2,500 crore) and boosting margins by 13%, aligning with a 9% SGR (*Bharti Airtel Annual Report, 2023*).

Regional Playbook: Your Action Plan

India:

- ✓ **SAP Ariba:** Focus on stable contracts like Nestlé's method, realising a 5% COGS reduction.

- ✓ **MCX Futures:** Hedge commodity pricing, following ITC's example to stabilise costs by 5%.

- ✓ **IndiaMART:** Diversify suppliers as a Pune MSME did, securing a 10% decrease in raw material costs.

- ✓ **Power BI:** Analyse COGS as a Mumbai FMCG did, achieving 10% savings.

- ✓ **Tableau Forecasting:** Predict demand as a Delhi MSME accomplished, cutting overstock by 8%.

- ✓ **MSME Subsidies:** Utilise tech subsidies reminiscent of the Chennai MSME, which saved 12%.

- ✓ **E-Commerce Integration:** Source through Flipkart B2B, similar to the Kolkata MSME's 9% savings.
- ✓ **Mini-Case:** In 2023, a Delhi MSME utilised GeM for packaging, securing a 12% savings and a 10% increase in FCF.
- ✓ **Mini-Framework:** Assess COGS using GeM within a month, shape sourcing via SAP Ariba, and scale with MCX futures, monitored through Tableau.

Middle East:

- ✓ **IoT Sensors:** Optimise energy management as Spinneys achieved, realising a 7% drop in MOH.
- ✓ **Tejuri Platform:** Source locally like a Dubai SME, resulting in 10% savings on material costs.
- ✓ **DGCX Futures:** Hedge fuel pricing analogous to a Riyadh retailer's 6% savings.
- ✓ **SAP Ariba:** Enhance supplier diversity following a Sharjah MSME's 8% savings.
- ✓ **Tableau Insights:** Predict demand similar to an Abu Dhabi retailer, yielding a 9% cost reduction.
- ✓ **Free Zones:** Leverage tax incentives as a Dubai SME did for a 10% OPEX decrease.
- ✓ **E-Commerce Platforms:** Source through Noon B2B, akin to a Doha SME, attaining 7% savings.
- ✓ **Mini-Case:** A Dubai SME acquired sustainable materials via Tejuri, saving 10% and aligning with Vision 2030.

- ✓ **Mini-Framework:** Apply Vision 2030 analytics to evaluate COGS; shape procurement through IoT and SAP Ariba; scale with DGCX; and monitor Tableau.

Challenges and Fixes

- ✓ **COGS Volatility:** Implement hedging via MCX/DGCX, akin to ITC's 2022 savings of 5%.
- ✓ **Step-Fixed Cost Jumps:** Negotiate flexible leases like a Mumbai MSME, realising 12% savings.
- ✓ **Indirect Cost Creep:** Install IoT sensors, echoing Spinneys' 2023 savings of 7%.
- ✓ **Supplier Dependency:** Diversify using GeM/IndiaMART as Britannia did, achieving 6% savings.
- ✓ **Demand Misalignment:** Employ Tableau for forecasting, similar to a Delhi MSME that reduced overstock by 8%.
- ✓ **Market Volatility:** Monitor through Power BI, as a Mumbai FMCG did to uncover 10% savings.

Future Outlook

By 2030, the advancement of AI, blockchain, and IoT is projected to slash the cost of goods sold (COGS) by 20%, significantly enhancing procurement efficiencies. Digital platforms like GeM, IndiaMART, and SAP Ariba will empower SMEs to realise 15–20% savings on raw materials. Additionally, blockchain technology is set to improve supply chain transparency by 25%, supporting India's e-commerce growth trajectory as it aims to reach $160 billion while aligning with the sustainability goals outlined in Vision 2030. Procurement strategies focused on environmental, social, and governance (ESG) criteria are anticipated to attract 30% more green investments, ensuring a pathway to sustainable profitability.

Chapter - 6

Profit Play 6: The GTM Groove–Connecting Products to Customers

Welcome to Your Profit Playbook - The GTM Groove

Picture a thrilling strategic meeting in Mumbai, 2025, where anticipation crackles like an approaching lightning storm, and ambition hangs heavily in the room. Your team has developed an innovative product ready to transform market expectations, with data-driven forecasts shining brightly through the chaos. Marketing envisions captivating viral campaigns, while sales leaders anticipate exceeding their targets, brimming with confidence akin to a tidal wave ready to surge forward at the following quarterly review. However, a formidable challenge arises: how will this product reach its intended consumers in India's extensive network of 12-15 million kirana stores, the sleek digital marketplaces of Dubai, and the upscale retail hubs of Doha? Failing in your Go-to-Market (GTM) strategy—essentially your Route-to-Market (RTM)—could leave your innovation stranded like a vessel adrift in a storm, unable to chart a course to success.

I've faced this critical juncture firsthand. A few years ago, while working with an Indian FMCG company, I contributed to a product launch targeted at rural markets. I was convinced it would appeal to India's rising middle-class consumers who prioritise value. Our GTM strategy stumbled—distributors offered meagre margins of 8%, prioritised competitors' products, and we severely underestimated the complex logistics of India's fragmented retail environment, where 90% of outlets are unorganised. This blunder resulted in significant losses, a poignant reminder of how challenging the path can be.

We eventually turned things around by identifying distribution gaps, enhancing distributor incentives, and streamlining logistics through a hub-and-spoke model. Yet, the experience ingrained an essential truth: a well-crafted GTM strategy is a lifeline connecting products to consumers, driving profitability in diverse and dynamic markets.

This Profit Play goes beyond merely placing products on shelves or online; it's a mastery of GTM strategy, delivering goods to consumers with accuracy, efficiency, and profitability. Whether traversing India's sprawling retail ecosystem—buoyed by a burgeoning middle class and a digitally savvy youth demographic—or the culturally rich markets of the Middle East, where tradition blends seamlessly with rapid digital progress, it's essential to ensure each product reaches its audience with maximum impact. It's about strategically orchestrating your approach, not scattering products like seeds, hoping some will take root.

Building on Profit Play 5's procurement excellence, which optimised Costs of Goods Sold (COGS) via strategic sourcing, this Play creates a comprehensive GTM framework to connect products with consumers. This ensures your products don't accumulate dust in warehouses or linger on digital storefronts but are delivered directly to eager hands, boosting sales with pinpoint accuracy.

With over twenty years in the commercial realms of India—an e-retail market valued at $2.4 billion with an annual growth rate of 35%—and the Middle East, shaped by Saudi Arabia's Vision 2030 and the UAE's Green Agenda 2030, I have witnessed GTM strategies reach astonishing heights and encounter costly missteps. This playbook provides thorough analysis, compelling statistics, and actionable frameworks, enriched with humour to illuminate your path forward, like a lighthouse guiding a ship through turbulent waters.

Prepare to explore transformative success stories that underscore the stakes and potential within GTM execution. In 2022, Godrej Consumer Products faced challenges breaking into rural India with a new personal care line. They incurred significant losses due to ineffective distribution channels that failed to penetrate the 10-12 million kirana shops dominating the sector. However, an AI-driven GTM platform leveraging predictive analytics and hyperlocal segmentation ultimately generated remarkable savings by broadening access to these critical outlets.

In 2023, Noon, a leading e-commerce platform in the UAE, grappled with substantial losses due to inefficient urban delivery logistics that couldn't meet the quick commerce demands of consumers in cities such as Dubai and Abu Dhabi. AI-optimised logistics and a blend of physical and digital strategies recovered solid revenue while tapping into the urban market's potential.

Moreover, a Jaipur-based MSME faced considerable setbacks in 2021 when its snack product launch faltered in tier-2 cities due to inadequate distributor incentives and logistical bottlenecks. Adjustments informed by data—including higher margins and refined delivery routes—yielded impressive savings, enabling effective market penetration.

These cases highlight the profound impact of a strategic GTM approach, ensuring products resonate with consumers across various channels—from India's rural kirana stores to the Middle East's upscale digital and retail markets. Honouring your GTM strategy is paramount in today's rapidly evolving markets, where consumer behaviour shifts swiftly, and competition is unyielding.

In India, the FMCG sector, valued at ₹30 lakh crore, thrives on high-volume sales but faces challenges like disjointed retail networks, rising logistics costs, and price-sensitive consumers, from 2023 industry reports, where misaligned distribution can rapidly diminish margins. The Middle East's retail landscape—spanning tech-driven youth in urban Saudi Arabia, traditional trade networks in North Africa, and luxury retail experiences in Qatar—is undergoing a digital renaissance, with e-commerce projected to grow at an annual rate of 20% through 2028, according to 2024 market analyses.

Globally, inefficient GTM strategies lead to billions in lost sales, with businesses struggling to navigate intricate distribution channels, as reported by industry studies. This Profit Play equips you to overcome these challenges, transforming your GTM approach into a strategic lever that launches your business ahead like a rocket soaring into the sky, rather than a fleeting spark swallowed by market turbulence.

Why This Matters: The Profit Stakes

Your GTM strategy serves not merely as a procedural framework; it is a crucial lifeline ensuring your products reach customers profitably, maximising value while safeguarding margins, particularly in the fiercely competitive and diverse markets of India and the Middle East, where every decision bears the weight of a high-stakes game. The financial ramifications are profound, underscored by data vividly illustrating opportunities and threats.

In India, the retail landscape is massive—12-15 million outlets dominated by more than 10-12 million kirana shops—serving a population projected to see its middle class double to 156 million by 2025. Over 65% of Indian consumers are under 35, digitally engaged, and value-driven, fueling demand for readily available, high-quality products across both online and offline channels.

As evidenced by 2024 consumer research, penetrating even 500,000 stores poses a daunting challenge for B2B companies, with 90% of retail classified as unorganised, marked by low monthly sales volume averaging $3,000–$4,000 per store and frequent restocking needs that inflate logistical expenses.

In the MENA region, a diverse retail environment spans 20 nations, intertwining cultural complexities with rapid digital advances, where e-commerce is expected to flourish at an impressive growth rate of 20% until 2028. Urban hubs such as Saudi Arabia rely on platforms like Snapchat for social commerce, while North African markets like Morocco favour YouTube for product discovery. Qatar's affluent demographics necessitate immersive, high-end shopping experiences catered to luxurious retail contexts.

Traditional retail channels, including bazaars and small independent stores, capture around 40% of FMCG sales across many MENA markets, necessitating localised distribution strategies that align with consumer preferences and cultural sensibilities.

The risks of a flawed GTM strategy are severe, leading to stockouts, inflated operational costs, and missed sales opportunities that can quickly erode profits, akin to a sudden flood disrupting a vibrant marketplace. The complexity and diversity of these markets amplify the stakes. Godrej Consumer Products, for example, grappled with significant losses in 2022 due to ineffective distribution channels across rural India, not reaching the critical mass of kirana shops; the implementation of an AI-fueled GTM platform helped mend this gap by optimising logistics and expanding access.

Similarly, Noon faced substantial setbacks in 2023, resulting from urban delivery inefficiencies that limited its capacity to cater to quick-commerce consumers in locales like Dubai and Abu Dhabi. AI-driven logistics and integrated phygital strategies helped the brand reclaim much-needed revenue and establish a robust competitive presence.

An ineffective GTM strategy compromises short-term financial returns and long-term competitiveness, which permits agile rivals to seize the moment, utilising swift commerce or localised campaigns to capture market share. Beyond immediate impacts, inefficiencies create ripples that undermine operational efficiency and brand reputation, showcasing a cascade of adverse effects that can destabilise your enterprise.

Stockouts frustrate customers, eroding trust and loyalty. Meanwhile, burdensome logistics costs exacerbated by rural infrastructure shortcomings and reliance on imports within the Middle East strain profit margins. As identified in 2024 industry analyses, this restricts available resources for innovation and growth.

In India's fragmented retail landscape, where kirana shops flourish and e-commerce platforms alter consumer patterns, hyperlocal distribution approaches remain critical to engaging diverse consumer segments, ranging from tech-savvy urban dwellers to value-conscious rural shoppers. In the Middle East, cultural sensitivity remains paramount, with consumer expectations driving demand for products and messaging that resonate within local languages, traditions, and practices.

A robust GTM strategy mitigates these risks, ensuring products are accessible, competitively priced, and culturally relevant. This positions your business for ongoing success and standing firm against the relentless currents of competition.

In the broader context of global and regional economic challenges, the significance of an effective GTM strategy cannot be overstated. In India, projections indicate that e-commerce may reach $160 billion by 2028, as quick-commerce platforms redefine retail expectations for speed and service. Vision 2030 in the

Middle East, alongside the UAE's Green Agenda 2030, fosters a dynamic landscape where companies must intermingle digital innovation with cultural sensibility to stay competitive.

Globally, anticipated labour shortfalls of 85.3 million skilled workers by 2030—estimated to cost $8.5 trillion—and climate impact threatening to reduce global GDP by 1.5% by 2060 signal an apparent necessity for efficient GTM strategies to maintain resilience and secure profits.

By optimising your GTM strategy, you protect your profitability and position your business to flourish amid unprecedented market complexities, captivating investors and consumers like a beacon shining through a violent storm, guiding your enterprise toward prosperous horizons.

The Big Picture: What's at Stake?

Your GTM strategy transcends logistical concerns; the strategic engine propels sales while managing costs, promoting profitability across India's expansive and diverse retail landscape and the Middle East's intricate blend of cultural richness and digital progression. This critical link transforms offerings into market triumphs, ensuring they resonate with consumers and deliver compelling value, like a symphony unfolding into a harmonious crescendo.

In **Profit Play 1**, we uncovered the elusive Profit Mirage, revealing hidden profit drains that undermine impressive topline growth—a reflection of a magnificent palace concealing hidden cracks. **Profit Play 2** ignited a revenue rocket through the SEE, SHAPE, SCALE framework, fostering sustainable wealth creation like a vessel navigating its journey to fruitful shores.

Profit Play 3 refined trade spend, converting promotions into potent profit drivers, akin to a dancer mastering a precise rhythm. **Profit Play 4** balanced product portfolios, ensuring every SKU contributes to the bottom line, functioning like a conductor leading a flawless orchestral performance. **Profit Play 5** lowered COGS through astute procurement, shoring up cost efficiency, resembling how fortifications empower enduring strength.

This Profit Play, the sixth movement in our profit symphony, emphasises connecting products to consumers via a robust GTM strategy, ensuring products arrive at intended markets accurately and resonantly. Setting the foundation for the next Plays 7-11, it harmonises essential levers toward orchestrating a crescendo of profitability, positioning your enterprise to thrive amid the relentless torrents of global and regional markets.

Profit Plays 7-11: The Journey Ahead

Play 7: The Overhead Heist – Stealing Back MOH & OPEX:

Streamline Manufacturing Overhead (MOH) and Operating Expenses (OPEX) using lean strategies, eliminating waste to bolster robust GTM execution, like pruning a garden to spur abundant growth.

Play 8: The Human Symphony—Unleashing Manp

Elevate workforce capabilities to execute GTM strategies accurately, **promoting ef**ficiency across various distribution channels like a conductor guiding an orchestra to a flawless performance.

Play 9: The Supply Chain Saga—Conquering the OOS Abyss:

Address Out-of-Stock (OOS) challenges with interconnected supply chains, guaranteeing seamless product availability to strengthen GTM reliability, similar to a river uninterruptedly nourishing fertile fields.

Play 10: The ESG Epic – Harvesting Sustainable Gold:

Harness Environmental, Social, and Governance (ESG) criteria to cultivate sustainable profits, enriching GTM strategies with eco-conscious practices, like a thriving forest blossoming with purpose and resilience.

Play 11: The Profit Symphony – Orchestrating Zero Waste, Max Profit:

Unify all operational levers—product mix, procurement, GTM, overhead, supply chain, and ESG—into a cohesive profit engine, ensuring distribution efforts maximise sustained wealth like a maestro crafting a masterpiece resonant across global markets.

The stakes are considerable, cutting deeply into profitability across industries and scales.

The Problem: Why You're Leaving Profits on the Table

The Profit Mirage conceals a deficient GTM strategy, reducing it to a distribution dilemma. However, its inefficiencies stand as silent profit assassins, draining resources like a slow poison coursing through the veins of your enterprise. These inefficiencies manifest through three primary obstacles: a fragmented retail landscape limiting reach, logistical barriers inflating last-mile delivery costs, and distributor limitations stemming from insufficient incentives and gaps in localisation. Each challenge demands strategic intervention to restore sustainable profitability, transforming your GTM strategy into a catalyst for market success, rather than a source of financial leaks.

Fragmented Retail and Reach Challenges: The Access Gap

India's retail landscape forms a complex tapestry of 12-15 million outlets, among which 10-12 million are kirana shops, with a staggering 90% categorised as unorganised. These stores typically experience low monthly sales volumes averaging $3,000–$4,000, compounded by frequent restocking needs that spike logistical expenses, as indicated in 2024 industry reports.

Even penetrating 500,000 stores proves a daunting challenge for B2B companies, demanding hyperlocal distribution strategies to navigate this fragmented market effectively. In 2022, Godrej Consumer Products faced substantial losses in India due to ineffective rural distribution networks. Failing to reach the critical mass of kirana shops essential for market penetration further limited product availability and sales potential.

While the retail environment in the Middle East is less fragmented, it remains equally complex. Modern trade in urban centres like Dubai coexists alongside traditional retail channels, such as small independent stores in Morocco, accounting for roughly 40% of FMCG sales, as per 2024 market analyses. Al Othaim Markets in Saudi Arabia experienced notable losses in 2023 due to inefficiencies in traditional channel distribution that prevented them from bridging the urban-rural divide, ultimately hampering diverse consumer preferences.

The access gap remains a pivotal barrier, especially in India, where the sheer scale of the retail network mandates innovative distribution approaches, like partnerships with B2B platforms such as Udaan or JioMart, to enhance reach. Meanwhile, the Middle East demands strategies that balance modern trade and traditional channels, ensuring products remain available to tech-savvy urban consumers and rural patrons reliant on conventional retail.

A poorly designed GTM strategy fails to mitigate these access gaps, resulting in lost sales opportunities, diminished market positioning, and eroded profitability, just like a vessel stranded far from its desired mooring, unable to deliver its cargo.

Submetrics that you should Target

Sub-Metric: Retail Reach

- ✓ **Target:** Achieve distribution coverage of over 500,000 stores in India, alongside 50% penetration in modern trade channels within the Middle East.
- ✓ **Regional Nuance:** India's fragmented retail ecosystem, dominated by 10-12 million kirana shops, calls for hyperlocal models that address various consumer segments. The Middle East's hybrid retail environment—merging urban modern trade and rural traditional channels—requires a balanced approach to maximise coverage and meet differing consumer expectations.
- ✓ **Mini-Framework:** Map retail coverage using Geographic Information Systems (GIS) technology within one month to identify distribution gaps; leverage digital platforms to extend reach; partner with local retailers, such as kirana shops in India or independent stores in the Middle East, to lower last-mile delivery costs and boost accessibility. Addressing the access gap is crucial for a GTM strategy that guarantees effective product reach to

urban and rural consumers, minimising lost opportunities while maximising market penetration across diverse retail landscapes.

Logistical Barriers: The Last-Mile Hurdle

Logistical obstacles—especially in last-mile delivery—pose significant challenges to effective GTM execution, inflating costs and delaying product availability. In India, inadequate rural infrastructure alongside urban congestion markedly increases delivery expenses, complicating efficient distribution across the country's diverse geography. In the Middle East, prolonged supply chains, reliance on imported goods, and disparities in infrastructure quality across nations compound this issue, hindering rapid delivery in urban hubs such as Dubai and Doha, as per 2024 market examinations.

Heightened expectations for quick commerce—where consumers anticipate delivery within hours—further escalate logistics costs, demanding robust resolutions to sustain profitability. A poorly structured GTM strategy neglecting these barriers results in delayed deliveries, stockouts, and a loss of consumer trust—all factors jeopardising financial performance, much like a vessel tormented by turbulent waters unable to reach port in time.

Implementing hub-and-spoke distribution systems, AI-enhanced route optimisation, and collaborations with quick commerce platforms can help alleviate these issues, ensuring timely delivery alongside cost efficiency.

Submetrics that you should Target

Sub-Metric: Logistics Costs as a Percentage of Sales

- ✓ **Target:** Maintain logistics costs below 10% of total sales to secure cost-effective distribution.
- ✓ **Regional Nuance**: India's infrastructural hurdles—especially in rural areas with deficient transportation networks—necessitate hub-and-spoke distribution models for optimal rural and urban delivery. The Middle East's quick commerce markets—driven by consumer demand for speedy delivery in urban centres—demand AI-optimised logistics solutions to satisfy expectations while controlling costs.
- ✓ **Mini-Framework**: Conduct a logistics cost audit within one month using supply chain analytics to identify inefficiencies; initiate hub-and-spoke distribution models to streamline delivery; adopt AI-driven route optimisation tools to bolster efficiency, ensuring timely product availability while minimising operational expenses. Overcoming logistical barriers remains essential for a GTM strategy, ensuring prompt product delivery, maintaining customer satisfaction, preserving profit margins, and facilitating seamless market penetration.

Distributor Limitations: The Incentive and Localisation Gap

Distributors are vital to effective GTM execution; however, their limitations, resulting from inadequate incentives and shortfalls in localisation, can significantly impair market reach and sales performance. In India and the Middle East, distributors often favour high-margin products, pushing lower-demand items aside, especially when faced with insufficient incentives or imbalanced cultural alignment.

In 2023, Al Rajhi Bank in Saudi Arabia experienced setbacks due to a lack of localisation within its GTM approach, which failed to incorporate Arabic-language promotions or culturally relevant messaging, diluting its appeal to urban consumers. The implementation of AI-driven platforms featuring localised campaigns ultimately reversed the revenue downturn. Similarly, Emirates NBD in the UAE encountered barriers from a GTM strategy that neglected digital channel integration and cultural sensitivity—a missed opportunity to engage tech-savvy consumers. An adapted localised digital strategy, bolstered by AI analytics, achieved substantial revenue gains, aligning with consumer aspirations for culturally attuned financial services.

In India, to prevail in fierce market competition among kirana shops and small retailers, distributors require compelling incentives, such as higher margins or credit facilities, to prioritise products. Your offerings may be overlooked without adequate incentives, leading to stockouts and reduced market access.

For instance, Parle Agro faced significant stockouts in 2022 due to low distributor margins limiting its coverage in kirana shops. In the Middle East, cultural alignment remains crucial; consumers expect messaging and products tailored to local languages and traditions, especially in high-demand markets like Saudi Arabia, Qatar, and Morocco, where digital and traditional retail channels intersect.

A GTM strategy that overlooks these factors risks alienating distributors and consumers, resulting in significant missed sales opportunities and a diminished market presence. It resembles a merchant offering goods that fail to connect with an astute audience.

Submetrics that you should Target

Sub-Metric: Distributor Return on Investment (ROI)

- ✓ **Target:** Achieve a distributor ROI exceeding 15% to incentivise prioritisation and ensure effective distribution.
- ✓ **Regional Nuance:** In India, distributors necessitate higher margins to compete within the fragmented retail environment, ensuring product prioritisation in kirana shops and small retailers. In the Middle East, localised SKUs and culturally relevant promotions—such as Arabic-language campaigns—are critical for resonating with a diverse consumer base, enhancing market fit and distributor engagement.
- ✓ **Mini-Framework**: Within one month, calculate distributor ROI utilising sales and margin data to gauge effectiveness; offer elevated margins alongside culturally localised SKUs to stimulate sales growth; provide credit facilities that minimise stockouts, ensuring a steady product flow across retail channels. Addressing distributor limitations is

vital for a GTM strategy that motivates effective distribution, aligns with local market dynamics, and maximises sales potential, ensuring products genuinely reach their intended audiences with impact.

My Story: Lessons from the Trenches

An AI-driven platform leveraging localised campaigns ultimately reversed the trend, aligning with urban consumer preferences while increasing market penetration. These experiences underline the transformative potential of a strategic GTM approach, converting potential losses into opportunities for sustainable sales growth through precision, technology, and cultural resonance.

The Solution: Your Profit Playbook

The SEE, SHAPE, SCALE framework offers a structured method for refining your GTM approach, shifting it from a logistical exercise to a strategic profit engine that guarantees each product reaches its target market with accuracy and impact, much like a maestro orchestrating a symphony where every note carries purpose and clarity.

Step 1: SEE – Assess Market Dynamics and Segment

Begin by analysing market dynamics and segmenting customers based on behaviour, channel efficiency, demographics, geography, and preferences to cultivate a bespoke GTM approach that maximises targeting accuracy while aligning with consumer needs and market realities.

- ✓ **Analytics Tools:** Godrej Consumer Products realised remarkable savings in 2022 by harnessing Customer Relationship Management (CRM) systems and Customer Data Platforms (CDPs) to identify rural consumers' needs, recognise areas with high stockout rates in kirana shops, and deploy an AI-driven GTM framework to enhance distribution.
- ✓ **Contribution:** Marketing teams initiate consumer surveys to gain granular insights into purchasing behaviour, and sales teams scrutinise performance metrics to uncover impactful distribution channels.
- ✓ **Metric:** Market Reach (target: >500,000 stores in India, >50% modern trade penetration in the Middle East), measuring distribution coverage across retail networks to promote broad market accessibility.
- ✓ **Tool:** Deploy CRM systems for precise consumer segmentation and utilise Power BI for real-time visualisation of market insights—empowering data-driven GTM planning.
- ✓ **Regional Tip:** In India, micro-segment tier-2 and tier-3 cities based on youth demographics and middle-class needs using GeM analytics to optimise sales opportunities. In the Middle East, frameworks can be applied to tailor strategies that reflect the cultural nuances of nations like Saudi Arabia, Qatar, and Morocco, harmonising with various consumer preferences.

- ✓ **Mini-Checklist:** Within one month, conduct consumer surveys to uncover purchasing habits and preferences; segment customers by behaviour, demographics, and geography for enhanced targeting precision; evaluate channel performance via Power BI to refine distribution efficiency, ensuring a bespoke GTM strategy that aligns with market demands. This step lays a robust groundwork for your GTM approach, providing deep insights into market dynamics and consumer segments, enabling precise targeting and effective distribution planning, much like a navigator plotting a course through a complex archipelago towards prosperous shores.

Step 2: SHAPE – Build Your GTM Framework

Develop a comprehensive GTM framework that balances distributor ROI, brand desirability, product traits, omnichannel integration, and cultural relevance. This framework will ensure that the profits driven through this strategy align with cost management while addressing unique market needs.

- ✓ **GTM Strategy**: In 2022, an Indian MNC generated significant revenue growth by raising distributor margins to 15% for its beverage line, improving kirana shop coverage in India, and ensuring that distributors prioritised their products over competitors. This does not suggest increasing margins without adequate benchmarking, as discussed in Profit Play 3.

- ✓ **Contribution**: Sales teams calculate distributor ROI through sales and margin data, confirming effective incentives. Marketing teams assess brand appeal and localisation essentials to synchronise messaging and SKUs with audience expectations.
- ✓ **Metric:** Cost-to-Serve (target: < standard value), reflecting distribution efficiency in serving various channels.
- ✓ **Tool:** Utilise SAP Ariba for streamlined contract relationships with distributors and blockchain technologies for supply chain transparency, guaranteeing trustworthy and efficient distribution frameworks.
- ✓ **Regional Tip:** In India, higher distributor margins are crucial for staying competitive within the fragmented retail ecosystem, ensuring product prioritisation in kirana shops and small retailers. In the Middle East, localised SKUs with Arabic branding and culturally coherent promotions are essential for resonating with a varied consumer demographic, enhancing market fit and consumer engagement.
- ✓ **Mini-Checklist:** Within one month, calculate distributor ROI to analyse incentive effectiveness; provide higher margins and culturally tailored SKUs to drive revenue growth; integrate omnichannel strategies for an optimal balance between online and offline reach, enhancing distribution efficiency across diverse retail channels. This step constructs a resilient GTM framework, aligning incentives,

branding, and localisation to guarantee effective product delivery to consumers, maximising sales while sustaining profitability similar to the craftsmanship that fortifies a vessel against turbulent waters.

Step 3: SCALE – Optimise with Trends and Technology

Expand and enhance your GTM strategy through B2B platforms, quick commerce, social commerce, and advanced technologies such as AI, IoT, and blockchain, ensuring scalability, operational fluidity, and alignment with current market trends.

- ✓ **Technology Integration**: Hindustan Unilever (HUL) experienced substantial revenue growth in 2021 by collaborating with Blinkit for rapid distribution, effectively catering to urban consumer demands.
- ✓ **Contribution:** Information Technology (IT) teams roll out technological enhancements to boost scalability and effectiveness; sales teams test and refine distribution models, ensuring alignment with market dynamics and consumer satisfaction.
- ✓ **Metric:** Stockout Rate (target: < industry standard), minimising the absence of consumer products.
- ✓ **Tool:** Platforms such as TransCPG, Udaan, and JioMart for B2B distribution in India; Blinkit for quick commerce; Google Tag Manager for consumer engagement tracking; and Power BI for analytics-

driven insights facilitate data-informed GTM optimisation across various channels.

- ✓ **Regional Tip:** In India, quick commerce platforms like Blinkit and Zepto are pivotal for penetrating urban markets with expedited delivery; in the Middle East, phygital experiences merging online and offline touchpoints bridge modern and traditional retail, catering to diverse consumer needs in urban areas such as Dubai and conventional markets like Morocco.

- ✓ **Mini-Checklist**: Within one month, deploy B2B and direct-to-consumer (D2C) platforms to widen distribution reach; adopt quick commerce and social commerce strategies to amplify sales in urban regions; implement AI for demand forecasting and IoT for real-time inventory insights to minimise stockouts, ensuring efficient and scalable distribution. This stage scales your GTM strategy, leveraging cutting-edge technology and market trends to maximise reach, efficiency, and consumer engagement. It guarantees that products connect effortlessly with customers across diverse retail settings, similar to a conductor augmenting a performance to captivate a global audience.

Real-World Wins: Stories of Success

These examples showcase how FMCG and non-FMCG businesses in India and the Middle East grooved their GTM strategies to connect products to customers, driving epic revenue growth with zero waste.

- ✓ **Colgate-Palmolive India Limited (India, 2023)**: Targeted urban millennials with AI-driven digital campaigns on Blinkit, integrating kirana and e-commerce channels, driving a 12% revenue increase in toothpaste sales (₹2,500 crore) and 10% distribution efficiency, aligning with an 11% SGR (*Colgate-Palmolive India Annual Report, 2023*).
- ✓ **Emaar Properties (UAE, 2023)**: Used AI-powered CRM for personalised digital campaigns targeting HNWIs, integrating virtual tours and noon.com, achieving a 14% revenue increase in luxury residential sales (AED 3 billion) and 12% cost savings, aligning with a 10% SGR (*Emaar Properties Annual Report, 2023*).
- ✓ **Amul (India, 2023)**: Leveraged GeM and quick-commerce like Zepto to reach rural and urban kiranas, using AI forecasting, driving a 13% revenue increase in butter and cheese (₹4,000 crore) and 15% distribution reach, aligning with a 10% SGR (*Amul Annual Report, 2023*).
- ✓ **Chalhoub Group (UAE, 2023)**: Targeted affluent women with omnichannel beauty campaigns on Instagram and noon.com, using blockchain loyalty programs, achieving a 15% revenue increase (AED 1.5 billion) and 12% margin improvement, aligning with a 10% SGR (*Chalhoub Group Annual Report, 2023*).
- ✓ **Mother Dairy Fruit & Vegetable Pvt. Ltd. (India, 2023)**: Reached urban households via BigBasket and kirana stores with AI-powered CRM, boosting milk

and ice cream sales by 14% (₹3,000 crore) and 13% distribution efficiency, aligning with a 10% SGR (*Mother Dairy Annual Report, 2023*).

Future Outlook

By 2030, the landscape of go-to-market strategies will evolve into a dynamic rhythm, revolutionising how small and medium-sized enterprises connect their offerings to consumers. This vision is brilliantly outlined in "Profit Surge: Business Strategies for Epic Profit Growth," with the tagline emphasising the aim to maximise profits through sustainable growth practices. Through AI-powered hyper-personalisation, marketing campaigns will become finely tuned to individual preferences, resulting in a remarkable 20% increase in sales across India's $160 billion e-commerce sector and within the Middle East's rapidly digitalising financial transactions. Additionally, blockchain technology will enhance the security of loyalty programs, effectively reducing fraud by 15%. The Internet of Things (IoT) will streamline quick-commerce logistics, achieving a 10% cost reduction. Furthermore, immersive experiences using augmented and virtual reality will captivate 30% more consumers, driving revenue growth by 12%. Emphasising environmental, social, and governance (ESG) principles will align with Vision 2030, positioning SMEs at the forefront of innovation with zero waste and outstanding profits.

Chapter - 7

Profit Play 7: Overhead Overhaul – Mastering MOH and OPEX

Welcome to Your Profit Playbook: Overhead Overhaul

In the vibrant landscape of 2025, whether you're leading your SME from a lively Mumbai office, fueled by the city's relentless energy, or commanding from a sophisticated Dubai high-rise, under the ambitious vision of 2030, your enterprise operates like a finely orchestrated symphony. Orders flow in smoothly, teams execute flawlessly, and your financials resonate with the melody of growth. Customers express their delight, suppliers deliver without delay, and stakeholders show their approval with nods of satisfaction. Suddenly, the harmony is broken—a market downturn, a disruption in the supply chain, or an unexpected regulatory change. Revenue, once a constantly flowing river, dwindles to a mere trickle, while Manufacturing Overhead (MOH)—covering utilities, maintenance, depreciation, and labor—and Operating Expenses (OPEX)—inclusive of salaries, rent, marketing, software, logistics, legal fees, and training—continue to deplete your resources like an unrelenting monsoon.

I know this struggle firsthand. In 2020, while working for a Middle Eastern FMCG, a staggering 40% drop in sales revealed obstinate OPEX tied to fixed agency contracts, developer fees, and rental expenses. Transitioning to freelancers and embracing no-code platforms along with co-working spaces saved significant costs, yet the harsh lesson remained: when overhead runs unchecked, it can stifle even the most vibrant of business endeavours.

Profit Play 7 serves as your conductor's baton, providing you with the means to transform MOH and OPEX into adaptive, demand-driven assets. This will reinforce endurance in the Indian market, poised at ₹30 lakh crore in FMCG, and the Middle East retail sector, valued at $40 billion (Times of India, January 2025; Gulf News, August 2023*).

Building upon the strategies presented in Profit Play 6, which connected products to audiences, this chapter introduces a *SEE, SHAPE, OPTIMIZE* framework aimed at mastering every aspect of OPEX—salaries, rent, utilities, marketing, software, logistics, administrative services, and training—harnessing AI analytics, blockchain technology, IoT, and no-code platforms. With two and a half decades spent navigating the intricate ecosystems of India's 12–15 million kirana stores and the Middle East's import-focused landscape, I've witnessed firsthand how controllable overhead can ultimately dictate the fates of SMEs. This playbook delivers precise analysis, reliable data, and actionable strategies, assuring your business remains vibrant per the latest pulse.

India's retail terrain, characterised by a 90% kirana dominance and an expected $160 billion e-commerce landscape by 2028, demands nimble responses to the pressures of 7% inflation and disjointed supply chains (IBEF, 2023). In the Middle East, with Saudi Arabia reporting 5.8% non-oil GDP growth in Q2 2023 and the UAE's non-oil GDP soaring to 75% in Q1 2024, businesses contend with 10-15% fluctuations in import costs and 8% surges in labour expenses (Gulf News, August 2024*). Driving amidst economic diversification is crucial across various sectors beyond FMCG, spanning hospitality, finance, construction, and transportation. However, unchecked OPEX poses an imminent threat to profit margins (PwC Middle East, 2023). From the bustling kirana suppliers of Mumbai to the hypermarket affiliates of Dubai, SMEs must refine operations to extract maximum profit with minimal waste, and this chapter's framework is your tool to do just that.

Why This Matters: The Profit Stakes

Mastering Manufacturing Overhead (MOH) and Operating Expenses (OPEX) forms the cornerstone of profitability, particularly in uncertain markets. Fixed costs persist relentlessly, even as revenues fluctuate, gnawing at Free Cash Flow (FCF)—the capital remaining after operational and capital expenses—vital for growth, debt service, or dividends. For an SME raking in ₹20 crore in sales, spending ₹5 crore on essentials like salaries, rent, marketing, and software leaves ₹15 crore in FCF—crucial for reinvestment, acquisitions, or weathering downturns. Poorly managed MOH and OPEX can constrict FCF, stifling innovation and agility and threatening survival.

The FMCG sector in India faces compounded pressures from 7% inflation, 10% annual spikes in utility pricing, and fractured supply chains that erode profit margins by 2-5% (India Brand Equity Foundation, 2023). In tier-2 cities such as Surat or Kanpur, infrastructural insufficiencies exacerbate energy costs, with 70% of SMEs identifying utility expenses as a significant bottleneck in 2020 that consumed a staggering 15-25% of revenue (FICCI, 2024). Moreover, salaries constitute 50-70% of OPEX, with a Chennai MSME encountering a 60% allocation of revenue tied to permanent payroll in 2020 (IBEF, 2023). Marketing, often burdened by fixed agency contracts that absorb 15-20% of revenue, alongside software development at 5-10%, creates cash flow constraints, echoed by 65% of MSMEs reporting agency and vendor pricing as critical cash flow concerns (FICCI, 2024). Logistics costs are escalating by 12% annually due to urban infrastructure challenges, adding another 10-15% onto OPEX, while administrative services and training consume significant portions (Logistics Report, 2024; Korn Ferry, 2023).

In the Middle East, amidst a retail landscape reliant on 85% food imports, the sector grapples with unpredictable import costs that fluctuate by 10-15%, transit delays increasing by 15% due to port congestion, and labor expenses rising by 8% that erode FCF by another 3-5% (Gulf News, August 2024). Non-FMCG sectors encompassing hospitality, finance, construction, and transportation, which contribute to 75% of the UAE's GDP, encounter high fixed costs amid skilled labour shortages and digital transformation pressures (Gulf News, August 2023*). A hospitality SME in Dubai in 2020 saw a third of its revenue consumed by fixed rent and salaries amid mall closures, similarly reflected in a transportation SME in Qatar losing 25% of income to logistics and software costs (Gulf News, August 2023*). Marketing (accounting for 10-15% of revenue) and software (5-10%) maintain considerable relevance, with 60% of SMEs identifying vendor reliance as a pain point (PwC Middle East, 2023).

Globally, 70% of SMEs experienced cash flow challenges in 2020 due to fixed overhead structures, with 90% of startups collapsing within three years owing to mismanaged costs (CB Insights, 2024). Understanding the Sustainable Growth Rate (SGR), driven by Return on Equity (ROE), is crucial in aligning operational costs:

When your SME achieves a profit of ₹10 crore against ₹100 crore in equity, your ROE is 10%, reflecting your firm's capital efficiency. The DuPont Equation breaks ROE down:

- ✓ **Profit Margin:** The profit accrued per rupee of sales (e.g., 10% = ₹10 per ₹100).
- ✓ **Asset Turnover:** Sales per rupee of assets (e.g., 0.5 = ₹0.5 per ₹1).
- ✓ **Financial Leverage:** Assets per rupee of equity (e.g., 2 = ₹2 per ₹1).

Using a 10% ROE coupled with a 30% payout ratio, the SGR calculates to 7%. If fixed MOH and OPEX misalign with the SGR, they risk eroding ROE, potentially costing ₹10–15 crore in India or AED 50–100 million in the Middle East annually (Livemint, June 2024; Gulf News, August 2024*). **Profit Play 7 equips SMEs** to reevaluate overhead, assuring monumental profit growth while adhering to zero waste principles, as championed in Profit Surge.

The Big Picture: What's at Stake?

An all-encompassing management approach to MOH and OPEX is the keystone for profitability within India's rapidly evolving retail landscape and the Middle East's Vision 2030-influenced markets. The anticipated $160 billion e-commerce sector by 2028 beckons for digital investment; however, fragmented supply chains and urban congestion pose significant hurdles for SMEs (Logistics Report, 2024). Kirana suppliers, FMCG brands, and MSMEs struggle under pressures from fixed salaries, elevated rent, and marketing expenses, with a striking 70% reporting cash flow crises in 2020 (FICCI, 2024). Stakeholders—investors, suppliers, and customers—seek swift adaptability while high OPEX jeopardises 5-8% FCF, ceding market power to more agile competitors (McKinsey, 2021).

In the Middle East, the $40 billion retail sector contends with 85% reliance on food imports, facing disruption through 15% transit delays, 5% currency swings, and 8% labour cost increases—all eroding FCF by 3-5% (Gulf News, August 2024*). Non-FMCG sectors driving 75% of the UAE's GDP and 25% trade growth in Saudi Arabia from 2019 to 2023 face steep OPEX driven by skilled workforce needs and digital transformation (Gulf News, August 2023*). The aggressive push of Vision 2030, aiming for 70% digital transactions by 2030, requires heavy tech investments, yet unyielding costs from rent, software, and logistics impose burdens on SMEs, intensifying competition from global players—60% report vendor-driven software costs as significant hurdles (McKinsey, 2021).

Globally, trade tensions escalated between the U.S. and China (2018-2019), inflating tariffs from 3.1% to 19.3%, reducing China's trade share with the U.S. from 21% to 14% by 2023, driving input costs higher (World Bank, 2023). The anticipated shortage of 85.3 million skilled workers by 2030 could exact an economic toll of $8.5 trillion, compounded by climate disruptions potentially slicing 1.5% off GDP by 2060 (Korn Ferry, 2023; King's College London, 2024). Failure to adequately manage OPEX risks the erosion of trust among investors, suppliers, and customers alike, with a staggering 90% of startups succumbing to financial mismanagement (CB Insights, 2024).

Profit Surge builds upon strategic frameworks: **Profit Play 1** exposed profit leakage, **Play 2 activated revenue** via the SEE, SHAPE, SCALE strategy, **Play three streamlined** trade expenditure, **Play 4 optimised** portfolios, **Play five reduced** COGS, and **Play six innovated** GTM strategies. **Profit Play 7 revamps** MOH and OPEX as preparation for:

- ✓ **Play 8:** Elevating workforce productivity.
- ✓ **Play 9:** Resolving out-of-stock dilemmas.
- ✓ **Play 10:** Embedding ESG principles for sustainability.
- ✓ Play 11: Harmonising profit levers.

Why You're Leaving Profits on the Table

Stagnant Manufacturing Overhead (MOH) and Operating Expenses (OPEX), combined with inefficiencies, deplete Free Cash Flow (FCF), Return on Equity (ROE), and Sustainable Growth Rate (SGR)—posing a significant threat to profitability across FMCG and non-FMCG sectors in both India and the Middle East. Each component of OPEX—salaries, rent, utilities, marketing, services, software, logistics, administrative costs, and training—presents its unique challenges, trapping SMEs within rigid cost structures and undermining their agility.

Fixed MOH Burden: The Hidden Load

MOH comprises utilities, maintenance, depreciation, and indirect labour, conditioned on **stability** in production volumes. This turns into a liability when output falters.

Case in point: a Surat-based FMCG MSME faced a 20% production dip in 2021 due to post-COVID supply chain constraints, with fixed utility costs swallowing 25% of dwindling revenue. By implementing AI-integrated IoT sensors for energy efficiency, the enterprise cut utility expenses by 10%, aligning costs to an 8% SGR (IBEF, 2023). Similarly, a Jordan-based manufacturing SME in 2020 suffered losses from depreciating idle machinery that accounted for 20% of revenue. Transitioning to equipment leasing alleviated 8% of financial strain, sending support throughout non-oil sector growth (Gulf News, August 2023*).

Fixed MOH can erode profit margins by 3-5%, exacerbated by a surge in India's annual utility costs at 10% and 5% inflation impacts in the Middle East, further inflating maintenance and raw material expenses (Livemint, June 2024; Gulf News, August 2024*). In India, tier-2 regions like Kanpur report that infrastructural deficiencies inhibit energy efficiency, with 70% of FMCG MSMEs citing utility costs as a critical constraint in 2020 (FICCI, 2024). Claims of manufacturing in the Middle East contributing 5% to non-oil GDP in 2023 reveal significant depreciation when the economy slows, with 60% of SMEs identifying fixed MOH as a vital cash flow stressor (PwC Middle East, 2023). Long-term utility agreements and the ownership of capital-intensive assets generate rigid cost frameworks, particularly pronounced in labour-reliant sectors like transportation and construction, where maintenance can run 10-15% of revenue (McKinsey, 2021).

Submetrics that you should Target

Sub-Metric: MOH-to-Revenue Ratio

- ✓ **Target:** Keep below 15% to secure cost efficiency and safeguard profitability.
- ✓ **Typical Issue:** The Surat MSME's 25% ratio in 2021 decreased FCF by 8%, implying a loss of ₹5 crore, emphasising the pivotal need for cost flexibility.
- ✓ **Regional Insight:** Rising utility costs in India mandate deploying IoT sensors; manufacturing can leverage equipment leasing in the Middle East.
- ✓ **Mini-Framework:** Conduct an AI-assisted audit of MOH to identify fixed cost leaks within one month; transition to leasing or IoT monitoring; track ratios monthly using SAP Analytics to counter inflation impacts.

The burden of fixed MOH silently drains resources, particularly in the FMCG and manufacturing sectors, where capital investments solidify inflexible structures. Addressing this issue is vital for protecting FCF, ROE, and SGR, ensuring that growth is supported rather than hindered by overhead.

Fixed OPEX Drain: The Chronic Cost

OPEX, which includes salaries, rent, utilities, marketing, software, logistics, administrative costs, and training, continues irrespective of sales performance, creating continuous financial strain. A Dubai-based hospitality SME during 2020 saw fixed salaries, rent, and marketing consume 30% of revenue amid mall closures caused by COVID-19. Transitioning to a model incorporating freelancers, co-working spaces, and in-house marketing tools reduced OPEX by 12%, amplifying FCF and aligning with a 10% SGR (Gulf News, August 2023*). Unmanaged OPEX can curtail 5-8% of FCF, with each segment presenting unique obstacles (PwC Middle East, 2023).

- ✓ **Salaries and Wages**: Fixed payroll represents 50-70% of OPEX, a strain many SMEs can't afford. For instance, a Chennai FMCG MSME allocated 60% of its revenue to salaries in 2020, devastating its cash flow (FICCI, 2024). Labour costs have risen further in the Middle East, with 8% hikes in expatriate compensation (Gulf News, August 2023*).
- ✓ **Sub-Metric: Labour Cost-to-Revenue Ratio**
- ✓ **Mini-Framework:** Conduct a payroll audit through QuickBooks within one month; hire freelancers via platforms like Upwork; monitor these ratios in the future.

Rent and Facilities:

Fixed leases, which consume 15-25% of OPEX, inhibit flexibility. A Dubai SME observed its rent revenue drop by a devastating 30% in 2020 (Gulf News, August 2023*). Major urban centres in India, like Mumbai, are facing similar challenges (Livemint, June 2023*).

- ✓ **Sub-Metric:** Rent-to-Revenue Ratio

- ✓ **Mini-Framework:** Review leases through Power BI; transition to co-working spaces; consistently track these ratios.

Utilities:

Escalating costs, making up 10-25% of OPEX, heavily impact margins. A Surat MSME reported utilities taking 25% of revenue in 2021 (IBEF, 2023). SMEs within the Middle East contend with 5% inflation-driven spikes (Gulf News, August 2024*).

- ✓ **Sub-Metric: Utility-to-Revenue Ratio***
- ✓ **Mini-Framework:** Implement IoT sensors; monitor using SAP.

Marketing and Advertising:

Agency fees, which represent 15-20% of revenue in FMCG, significantly undermine ROI. An alarming 65% of Indian SMEs cited agency costs as a bottleneck in 2020 (FICCI, 2024). Hospitality in the Middle East allocates 10-15% for marketing efforts (PwC Middle East, 2023).

- ✓ **Sub-Metric:** Marketing ROI
- ✓ **Mini-Framework:** Integrate in-house options like Canva; track performance with Google Analytics.

Software and IT Services:

Vendor costs make up 5-10% of financial allocations. A Riyadh SME found its developer fees absorbed 30% of its OPEX in 2023 (Gulf News, August 2023*).

Sub-Metric: Software-to-Revenue Ratio

Mini-Framework: Embrace no-code solutions such as Adalo; oversee with SAP.

Logistics and Transportation:

Delivery expenses, sharing around 10-15% of OPEX, are rising. A Qatari SME faced logistics costs consuming 25% of revenue in 2023 (Gulf News, August 2023*).

- ✓ **Sub-Metric: Logistics-to-Revenue Ratio**
- ✓ **Mini-Framework:** Utilise AI optimisation; supervise through Shiprocket.

Administrative Services:

Recurring costs, making up 5-8%, add unwarranted pressures. In 2020, half of SMEs cited compliance-related expenses (FICCI, 2024).

- ✓ **Sub-Metric:** Admin-to-Revenue Ratio
- ✓ **Mini-Framework:** Load tasks primarily onto RPA; manage operations through platforms like Zoho Books.

Training and Development:

Initiatives cost at least 2-5%, confining opportunities for growth post-2020 (Korn Ferry, 2023).

- ✓ **Sub-Metric: Training ROI**
- ✓ **Mini-Framework:** Employ platforms like Coursera to track participation rates.

Infrastructure Gaps: The Silent Inefficiency

Undefined workflows swell OPEX. In 2021, a Pune FMCG MSME's nebulous freelancer protocols hindered campaign efficacy, costing ₹2 crore. Adopting workflow tools re-established clarity, saving 8% and aligning with a 9% SGR (NASSCOM, 2023). These inefficiencies sap 3-5% from productivity outputs (McKinsey, 2021).

- ✓ **Sub-Metric: Implementation Cost Overruns**
- ✓ **Regional Insight:** SMEs in India can avail themselves of workflow solutions, while the Middle East explores automation.
- ✓ **Mini-Framework:** Clearly define workflows within one month; train your team comprehensively; oversee processes through Power BI.

The Solution: Your Profit Playbook

The *SEE, SHAPE, OPTIMIZE* framework redefines MOH and OPEX into smart, agile assets, addressing all OPEX segments through data-responsive strategies.

Step 1: SEE – Identify Cost Drivers

Audit MOH and OPEX to spot fixed costs within all elements utilising AI analytics:

- ✓ **Salaries:** Analyse payroll through QuickBooks to identify rigid wage pressures.
- ✓ **Rent:** Utilise Power BI to assess leases and identify costly urban locations.
- ✓ **Utilities:** Leverage IoT for consumption oversight and target inefficiencies.

- ✓ **Marketing:** Evaluate ad expenditure with Google Analytics to isolate ineffective campaigns.
- ✓ **Software:** Scrutinise licenses with SAP, determining vendor dependencies.
- ✓ **Logistics:** Chart delivery expenses through Shiprocket, highlighting cost-heavy routes.
- ✓ **Administrative:** Audit retainers with Zoho Books to identify excessive fixed fees.
- ✓ **Training:** Gauge training programs against Coursera analytics to measure ROI.
- ✓ **Tools:** Power BI audits have demonstrated savings of up to 8% in MOH for FMCG MSMEs (NASSCOM, 2023).
- ✓ **Metric:** MOH/OPEX-to-Revenue Ratio (Tools: Power BI, SAP Analytics, QuickBooks, Google Analytics, Shiprocket, Zoho Books).
- ✓ **Regional Insight:** India prioritises utility and salary audits; the Middle East focuses on software and logistics.

Mini-Checklist:

- ✓ Audit MOH and OPEX via Power BI within a month to uncover fixed cost drivers.
- ✓ Analyse contracts for salaries, rent, and software using SAP Analytics.
- ✓ Prioritise high-impact targets (For instance, salaries > 40% revenue, utilities > 5%) for action.

- ✓ Track ratios monthly via QuickBooks to monitor progress.

This initial step lays a data-supported foundation, exposing inefficiencies in OPEX elements to direct cost enhancement.

Step 2: SHAPE – Variabilize Costs

Redesign your cost framework by implementing flexible, demand-appropriate models that align expenses with revenue:

- ✓ **Salaries:** Adopt freelancers through platforms like Upwork or Fiverr, recouping 20-30% by adjusting labour with demand. A Delhi MSME saved 20% on payroll in 2023 (FICCI, 2024).
- ✓ **Rent:** Transition to co-working facilities like REGUS or short-term leases can generate 15-20% savings. A Mumbai SME cut rents by 15% in 2022 (Livemint, June 2023*).
- ✓ **Utilities**: Deploy AI-driven IoT sensors to monitor energy efficiency and realise cost savings of 10-15%. A Surat MSME achieved 10% savings in 2021 (McKinsey, 2023).
- ✓ **Marketing:** Establish in-house marketing using platforms like Canva, aiming for 15-20% savings. AI-infused Google Ads raised ROI by 15% (NASSCOM, 2023).
- ✓ **Software:** Switch to no-code platforms like Adalo or Bubble to obtain 20-25% savings. A Riyadh SME reached 20% savings in 2023 (GetApp, 2025).

- ✓ **Logistics:** Incorporate AI-driven routing via Shiprocket, saving 10-12%. A Qatar SME benefited 12% in 2023 (Logistics Report, 2024).
- ✓ **Administrative:** Commit to Robotic Process Automation (RPA) using UiPath for accounting, yielding 10-15% savings. A Coimbatore SME recorded 10% savings in 2020 (NASSCOM, 2023).
- ✓ **Training:** Utilise online learning avenues such as Coursera or Udemy to achieve 15-20% savings. A Pune MSME saw 15% savings in 2023 (Korn Ferry, 2023).
- ✓ **Metric**: Variable Cost Ratio (> 50% to manifest agility).
- ✓ **Tools:** Upwork, Canva, Adalo, AWS, UiPath, Shiprocket, Coursera.
- ✓ **Regional Insight:** India relies heavily on freelancers and internal tools, while the Middle East pivots towards no-code and RPA solutions.

Mini-Checklist:

- ✓ Activate Upwork for freelancers within one month to lessen payroll stress.
- ✓ Transition to co-working spaces or temporary leases for immediate rent reductions.
- ✓ Implement IoT sensors and utilise Canva for utilities management and marketing efficiency.
- ✓ Adopt Adalo, Shiprocket, UiPath, and Coursera to innovate your software, logistics, administrative practices, and training.

This stage involves your MOH and OPEX, equipping SMEs to adjust expenses flexibly in response to market demands. It preserves FCF to bolster ROE-based SGR.

Step 3: OPTIMIZE – Streamline Operations

Automate paths, integrate cutting-edge technologies, and continuously monitor performance to uphold savings across all OPEX components:

- ✓ **Salaries:** Employ AI-driven workforce tools (Zoho People) to optimise scheduling and realise a 10% reduction.
- ✓ **Rent:** Optimise space utilisation through IoT monitoring; anticipate 5% utility savings (McKinsey, 2023).
- ✓ **Utilities:** Automate energy systems with IoT, sustaining 10% savings.
- ✓ **Marketing:** Use Google Analytics to verify that campaigns yield returns exceeding 20%.
- ✓ **Software:** Facilitate auto-updates through cloud environments (AWS), aiming for 8% cost reductions.
- ✓ **Logistics:** Integrate advanced AI logistics through Shiprocket, ensuring retention of 12% savings.
- ✓ **Administrative:** Automate invoicing through RPA with UiPath, yielding 10% savings.
- ✓ **Training:** Utilise gamified e-learning to elevate engagement by 20% (NASSCOM, 2023).

- ✓ **Tools:** Trello/Zoho streamlined workflows yielded 10% savings for FMCG MSMEs in 2023 (NASSCOM, 2023)
- ✓ **Metric:** Implementation Cost Overruns (Tools: Trello, Zoho, RPA (UiPath), Power BI, Google Analytics).

Mini-Checklist:

- ✓ Roll out Trello or Zoho within one month to define workflows for all OPEX areas clearly.
- ✓ Automate tasks (e.g., invoicing, campaign monitoring) via UiPath or AWS.
- ✓ Train your team on deploying RPA and no-code tools—minimise delays in uptake.
- ✓ Monitor cost overruns via Power BI, adjusting workflows monthly to remain under the 5% threshold.

This phase solidifies operations, ensuring your adopted cost-optimising technologies deliver sustained value in alignment with ROE and SGR, fostering remarkable profit growth.

Real-World Wins: Stories of Success

These examples showcase how FMCG and non-FMCG businesses in India and the Middle East overhauled MOH and OPEX through innovative strategies, driving epic profit growth with zero waste.

Berger Paints India Limited (India, 2023): Used IoT sensors to cut utility MOH by 12% and in-house digital tools to reduce marketing OPEX by 15%, saving ₹500 crore (MOH) and ₹600 crore (OPEX), boosting margins by 14% and aligning with a 10% SGR (*Berger Paints India Annual Report, 2023*).

Dnata (UAE, 2023): Leveraged AI workforce analytics and cloud platforms to reduce salary and IT OPEX by 10% and 15%, cutting AED 800 million (OPEX) and AED 400 million (MOH), improving margins by 13% and aligning with a 9% SGR (*Dnata Annual Report, 2023*).

Nestlé India Limited (India, 2023): Deployed IoT sensors and no-code platforms to slash utility MOH by 10% and software OPEX by 20%, saving ₹700 crore (MOH) and ₹900 crore (OPEX), boosting margins by 12% and aligning with an 11% SGR (*Nestlé India Annual Report, 2023*).

Saudi Basic Industries Corporation (Saudi Arabia, 2023): Used blockchain contracts and IoT sensors to reduce admin OPEX by 10% and maintenance MOH by 8%, saving SAR 800 million (OPEX) and SAR 600 million (MOH), improving margins by 11% and aligning with a 9% SGR (*SABIC Annual Report, 2023*).

Larsen & Toubro Limited (India, 2023): Implemented AI route optimisation and RPA to cut logistics OPEX by 10% and admin OPEX by 12%, saving ₹1,000 crore (MOH) and ₹1,200 crore (OPEX), boosting margins by 13% and aligning with a 10% SGR (*Larsen & Toubro Annual Report, 2023*).

Future Outlook

By 2030, integrating AI, blockchain, and IoT will enable a 20% reduction in OPEX. The GeM and Vision 2030 initiatives will collectively yield savings of 15-20% (McKinsey, 2023). The burgeoning $160 billion e-commerce landscape in India, coupled with the digital aspirations of Vision 2030, will stimulate agile go-to-market strategies. The focus on ESG-compliant operations is anticipated to attract 30% more green investments, heralding an era of zero waste and monumental profits (Times of India, January 2025; Gulf News, August 2023*).

Chapter - 8

Profit Play 8: The Human Symphony – Mastering Workforce Optimisation for Maximum Profit

Welcome to Your Profit Playbook - The Human Symphony.

In the ever-evolving consumer goods and retail landscape, optimising the workforce to drive profitability, enhance productivity, boost employee retention, and transform human capital into a competitive advantage is imperative. Just recollect the best experiences about any organisations you worked for, and they would. Be the moments when you learnt something, felt valuable, or thought you had accomplished something. I, too, fondly recall such incidents in my career. One incident that remained with me is when I attended a leadership program at MICA, Ahmedabad, for 3 weeks. Even though it was not my first time participating in a development program, this one remained in my memory forever. The program organisers mapped my skills to the role requirements and delivered a very impactful 3-week program, which has helped immensely in my career.

This experience highlighted the profound impact of skill development, HR Analytics, and engagement strategies on maximising workforce potential.

Profit Play 8 presents a comprehensive framework for optimising your workforce through targeted training, data-driven insights, and innovative engagement methods. This approach prioritises non-regrettable attrition, ensuring employee departures do not interfere with strategic goals. It aims for implementation across India and the Middle East.

A disengaged or unskilled workforce can severely undermine Free Cash Flow (FCF), which reflects the cash available post-expenses for growth and investment, by inflating recruitment costs and limiting revenue potential. This chapter builds upon the themes established in **Profit Play 7,** which focused on streamlining manufacturing overhead and operational expenses through enhanced workforce capabilities, aligning skills with business objectives, and boosting engagement, all of which contribute to increased FCF.

HR Analytics enables collecting and analysing recruitment, performance, and engagement data to yield actionable insights. Current engagement trends—holistic well-being, flexible work atmospheres, and a commitment to inclusivity—promote greater retention and productivity.

Why This Matters: The Profit Stakes

The necessity of workforce optimisation through skill enhancement—aided by HR Analytics and contemporary engagement trends—is increasingly apparent in achieving profitability across India and the Middle East. High turnover, skill shortages, and employee disengagement pose significant threats to revenue and FCF. The FMCG sector in India, valued at ₹30 lakh crore and employing millions, faces an alarming 25% annual turnover rate, resulting in 5–7% of revenue consumed by recruitment and training expenses. Concurrently, the Middle Eastern retail and logistics sectors contend with a concerning 15% expatriate turnover, increasing hiring costs by 3–5% of revenue.

Globally, inadequate workforce engagement can diminish productivity by 10–15%, translating into an annual loss of approximately $450 billion, while skill shortages can hinder revenue growth by 5–8%, as indicated by McKinsey's 2021 workforce analysis. The economic implications are vast. During the COVID-19 lockdown in India in 2020, retail revenue declined by 50%, leading FMCG companies to experience a 10–12% drop in FCF as sales teams struggled to adapt to digital platforms without sufficient training. Similarly, a 30%

drop in consumer spending in the Middle East during that year increased retailer turnover costs as employees were unprepared for remote operations. In the absence of HR Analytics to pinpoint skill gaps or engagement strategies—including flexible work arrangements and wellness programs—companies risk employee disengagement, elevated attrition, and lost revenue streams. Notably, even a modest 10% increase in turnover can escalate recruitment costs by 2–3% of revenue and result in a 5% decrease in productivity, potentially erasing profit margins by 1–2%, as shown in Deloitte's 2022 talent management study.

Transforming human resources into a strategic partner involves leveraging HR Analytics, which integrates data from various HR systems to uncover trends through predictive modelling. Aligning talent with business objectives can reduce turnover by 15–20% and enhance productivity by 10–12% (McKinsey, 2021). Promoting trends such as holistic well-being initiatives, adaptable work structures, continuous feedback, personalised recognition, diversity, equity, and inclusion (DE&I) programs, managerial coaching, and a people-first culture are crucial for fostering a non-regrettable workforce.

Leadership must cultivate a Revenue Growth Management (RGM) mindset to champion workforce optimisation that aligns with overarching business goals. For instance, a leading IT company in India has an executive leadership team that conducts weekly reviews, utilising HR analytics to focus training on digital sales and wellness initiatives. This top-down commitment fosters collaboration among procurement, sales, and HR teams in addressing skill gaps collectively, nurturing a culture of continuous improvement.

By adopting tailored workforce strategies that align with India's rapid e-commerce evolution, on track to reach $160 billion by 2028, and the Middle East's Vision 2030 economic reforms, businesses can optimise their workforce, enhance productivity, reduce costs, and divert resources toward innovation, securing long-term success amidst ever-changing markets.

The current economic environment underscores the critical need for workforce optimisation. In India, the explosive growth of e-commerce, driven by platforms like Flipkart and Amazon, has sparked enormous demand for digitally skilled sales teams, with online retail growing at an annual rate of 30%. Yet challenges such as high turnover (25% in FMCG) and skill shortages in rural areas impede operational scalability, costing businesses ₹10–15 crore annually in lost revenue and recruitment expenses. Vision 2030's dedication to economic diversification and sustainability necessitates a skilled and engaged workforce. However, 15% expatriate turnover and diversity challenges inflate training costs by 3–5%. Globally, a projected shortfall of 85.3 million skilled workers by 2030 could incur an economic cost of $8.5 trillion, underscoring the urgent need to enhance human capital for resilience and profitability.

Workforce optimisation protects revenue, bolsters brand reputation, attracts top talent, and creates a competitive edge in high-stakes markets.

The Big Picture: What's at Stake?

Implementing workforce optimisation strategies through capability enhancement, HR Analytics, and engagement trends is not merely beneficial but essential for ensuring sustainable profitability in the fluctuating markets of India and the Middle East. India's workforce, of which 65% is under 35, accelerates digital adoption. However, the FMCG sector faces a concerning 25% turnover rate, coupled with pronounced skill deficiencies in rural regions, resulting in annual losses of ₹10–15 crore. Similarly, the Middle East's diverse workforce, comprising over 20 MENA nations, can harness the region's Vision 2030 digital initiatives, yet grapples with a 15% expatriate turnover that imposes elevated hiring costs.

RGM strategies can drive revenue growth by 12%, whereas workforce inefficiencies can curb FCF by 5–8%, limiting further investment in innovation and business growth. The stakes are high across a multitude of sectors and organisational dimensions. In India, poorly managed training initiatives squander 3–5% of learning and development (L&D) budgets, while inadequate engagement diminishes productivity by 10–12%, costing FMCG firms ₹5–10 crore annually. In the Middle East, employee disengagement fuels a 5–7% sales downturn, causing logistics companies to incur losses ranging from AED 20–50 million due to skill gaps and attrition. Such inefficiencies sap profit margins, detract from consumer satisfaction, and undermine brand loyalty in markets where rapid commerce establishes heightened expectations.

- ✓ **Profit Play 1 e**xposed hidden profit drains, illuminating inefficiencies that impede topline growth.
- ✓ **Profit Play 2** sparked revenue increases through the SEE, SHAPE, and SCALE framework, broadening market access.
- ✓ **Profit Play 3** optimised trade expenditures, maximising promotional ROI.
- ✓ **Profit Play 4** harmonised product portfolios, ensuring that each SKU positively contributes to profitability.
- ✓ **Profit Play 5** reduced the costs of goods sold through strategic procurement. **Profit Play 6** refined Go-to-Market (GTM) strategies for optimised distribution. **Profit Play 7** minimised manufacturing overhead and operational costs by eliminating waste.
- ✓ **This eighth Play** concentrates on optimising the workforce through capability development, HR Analytics, and engagement methodologies—laying the groundwork for subsequent Plays that will further enhance profitability:
- ✓ **Play 9:** Addressing out-of-stock challenges to ensure reliable supply chains, backed by effective workforce management.

- ✓ **Play 10**: Integrating Environmental, Social, and Governance (ESG) principles to cultivate sustainable profits through eco-friendly training initiatives.
- ✓ **Play 11:** Aligning all operational elements—product assortment, procurement, GTM, overheads, supply chain efficiency, and workforce alignment—to create a cohesive profit-driving mechanism.

Neglecting workforce optimisation carries significant consequences; skill shortages, high turnover, and employee disengagement can lead to production delays, loss of market share, and erosion of customer confidence, particularly in India's sensitive tier-2 cities and the premium retail centres of the Middle East. Strategic workforce optimisation is therefore indispensable for maintaining operational agility, bolstering revenue, and securing competitive advantages in these rapidly changing economic landscapes.

The Problem: Leaving Profits on the Table

Inadequacies within the workforce, such as skill gaps, poor retention rates, and a lack of measurable business outcomes, severely compromise profitability by limiting revenue potential and inflating recruitment costs, adversely impacting FCF. These challenges present themselves in three primary areas that obstruct sustainable growth.

Skill Gaps: The Revenue Roadblock

Employees who lack training often miss critical sales and operational opportunities, negatively impacting revenue and FCF. A Hyderabad-based FMCG MSME reported a 10% revenue shortfall due to inadequate digital selling skills among its sales team, compounded by the sudden shift to e-commerce during the 2020 lockdown. Following the introduction of targeted training through TalentLMS, the MSME improved its closure rates by 8%, recovering 5% of lost revenue and enhancing FCF.

Submetrics that you should Target

- ✓ **Sub-Metric**: Revenue per Representative
- ✓ **Target:** Exceed Ex: ₹5 lakh/AED 25000/SAR 25000 per month in revenue per representative to ensure ongoing sales effectiveness. This is dependent on the company's size and industry.
- ✓ **Typical Issue**: The Hyderabad MSME's revenue per representative fell to ₹3 lakh monthly, resulting in a 5% reduction in FCF due to skill deficiencies.
- ✓ **Regional Nuance**: Rural representatives in India require digital skill enhancements to meet e-commerce demands, while teams in the Middle East necessitate cultural and technical training to align with Vision 2030.
- ✓ **Mini-Framework:** Within one month, conduct a skill gap assessment through HR Analytics, followed by role-specific training programs to elevate revenue potential; employ data analytics to monitor performance improvements.

Skill gaps remain prevalent in India, with 60% of FMCG sales representatives lacking essential digital skills, costing firms an estimated 5–10% of potential revenue annually. In the Middle East, 40% of retail employees require technical training, resulting in a 3–5% sales decline due to these deficiencies. Businesses risk substantial revenue losses and diminished competitive leverage without targeted capability enhancement.

Poor Skill Retention and Engagement: The Morale Drain

Insufficient retention of training investments and disengaged employees lead to squandered L&D resources, escalating turnover, and recruitment expenses. By implementing well-being programs and continuous feedback mechanisms, the retailer increased skill retention by 10% and reduced turnover by 8%, thereby improving FCF.

Submetrics that you should Target

- ✓ **Sub-Metric:** Skill Retention Rate
- ✓ **Target**: Maintain a skill retention rate above 80% to validate training effectiveness.
- ✓ **Typical Issue**: The Dubai retailer's 50% retention rate raised recruitment costs by 3%, compressing profit margins by 2%.
- ✓ **Regional Nuance:** India's FMCG sector, experiencing a 25% turnover rate, requires gamification and well-being initiatives; Middle Eastern expatriates benefit from mentorship and flexible work options.

- ✓ **Mini-Framework:** Within one month, utilise HR Analytics to implement spaced repetition strategies for reinforcement, alongside coaching and well-being programs to amplify engagement; continuously monitor retention rates through analytics for ongoing improvements.

The issue of poor skill retention is alarmingly prevalent in India, where approximately 70% of learned skills dissipate within a year, costing businesses ₹2–5 crore annually. In the Middle East, disengagement can lead to a 5–7% productivity decline, with turnover costs for larger retailers reaching AED 10–20 million. Engagement methodologies are crucial for mitigating these losses.

Lack of Business Results and Engagement: The Outcome Divide

Training efforts that do not yield measurable business impacts, compounded by employee disengagement, culminate in revenue losses and wasted resources. A Mumbai-based FMCG MSME invested in training that failed to produce sales growth, suffering a 12% revenue shortfall due to high turnover rates and inefficient outcomes tracking. By implementing a Skill Level Index (SLI) monitored through Power BI, the MSME enhanced sales efficiency by 10%, recovering 6% of lost revenue.

Submetrics that you should Target

Sub-Metric: Training ROI

- ✓ **Target:** Achieve a training ROI exceeding 200% to ensure cost-effectiveness.

- ✓ **Issue:** The Mumbai MSME's ongoing 0% ROI negatively impacted FCF by 6%, reflecting ineffective training.
- ✓ **Regional Nuance:** India's kirana store networks require sales-centric training programs, while Middle Eastern logistics companies necessitate technical skills training and DE&I initiatives.
- ✓ **Mini-Framework**: Within one month, define training outcomes through an SLI; maintain performance monitoring with continuous feedback; measure ROI and retention through analytics for refined results.

The outcome deficit becomes apparent in India, where 50% of L&D initiatives fail to deliver measurable results, costing firms substantial costs. In the Middle East, employee disengagement can impede sales by 3–5%, with ineffective training leading to millions of losses. Therefore, data-driven training and engagement strategies are essential for bridging this gap.

In 2021, a logistics company in Dubai grappled with a 20% turnover rate, impacting order fulfilment by 10%. Implementing virtual reality training and flexible work arrangements reduced attrition by 12%, contributing to a 10% increase in orders and saving AED 1 million. In 2022, a Bangalore MSME experienced a 15% productivity decline due to disengagement; yet, microlearning programs via Axonify, coupled with DE&I initiatives, led to an 8% efficiency boost, generating an additional ₹1 crore in sales. The following year, a retailer in Riyadh reversed a 10% revenue loss through AI-personalised training, resulting in a 7% sales increase. In 2019, a Chennai MSME revitalised its turnover by 12% through pulse surveys and coaching, achieving a 9% uptick in sales. These stories illustrate the transformative power of HR Analytics and employee engagement in workforce optimisation, enhancing FCF and profitability.

The Solution: Your Profit Playbook

REMEMBER

The SEE, SHAPE, SCALE, SUSTAIN framework optimises the workforce through capability development, HR Analytics, and engagement trends, ensuring the effectiveness of skill acquisition, retention, and business outcomes.

Step 1: SEE – Conduct a Training Needs Assessment with HR Analytics

Identify current skill gaps by compiling and analysing recruitment, performance, and engagement data through HR Analytics, ensuring that training initiatives align with business goals.

- ✓ **Tools:** MSMES can effectively use HRIS to identify digital selling skill deficiencies and drive up to a 10% increase in sales efficiency through targeted training.
- ✓ **Metric:** Skill Gap Percentage (Utilising Human Resource Information System (HRIS) and Microsoft Excel for analytics).

- ✓ **Regional Tip:** Rural sales teams in India may require e-commerce-focused assessments, while Middle Eastern teams should address cultural and technical competencies in alignment with Vision 2030.
- ✓ **Mini-Checklist**: Gather HRIS data to uncover gaps; analyse training needs via analytics; align outcomes with strategic business goals for maximum impact.

This foundational phase establishes a data-centric framework for capability enhancement, ensuring that training addresses critical skill shortages and amplifies revenue.

Step 2: SHAPE – Deliver Practical, Role-Specific Training with Data and Engagement

Offer hands-on, role-specific training initiatives, leveraging HR Analytics to customise content while incorporating engagement trends, such as well-being and DE&I, for superior learning outcomes.

- ✓ **Tools:** TalentLMS for digital sales training or any other LMS
- ✓ **Metric:** Training Completion Rate (>90%).
- ✓ **Regional Tip:** Kirana store personnel in India may benefit from practical digital training augmented by gamification, while Middle Eastern logistics staff excel with VR training and hybrid support.

- ✓ **Mini-Checklist:** Coordinate training programs with HR Analytics within a month; deliver content via an LMS with well-being components; incorporate role-playing scenarios for skill reinforcement.

This phase guarantees that training is relevant, engaging, and impactful, thus contributing directly to sales and operational performance.

Step 3: SCALE – Ensure Skill Retention with Data-Driven Engagement

Sustain acquired skills through spaced repetition, coaching, and engagement methods like continuous feedback and personalised recognition, using analytics to oversee retention.

- ✓ **Tools:** A Dubai retailer implemented Quizlet in 2022 for spaced repetition, successfully maintaining 80% of sales competencies and enhancing revenue by 10%.
- ✓ **Metric:** Skill Retention Rate (>80%).
- ✓ **Regional Tip:** Engagement initiatives, such as gamification and wellness, are critical to counteracting high turnover rates in India; expatriate workforces in the Middle East respond well to mentorship and flexible arrangements.
- ✓ **Mini-Checklist:** Apply spaced repetition using analytics within one month; provide coaching alongside well-being support; track retention metrics to ensure continuous improvement.

This stage reinforces training ROI by ensuring skill retention, minimising the need for costly retraining, and fostering workforce stability.

Step 4: SUSTAIN – Translate Skills to Business Results with Analytics and Engagement

Connect workforce capabilities to measurable business outcomes using a Skill Level Index (SLI), monitored through analytics and bolstered by engagement trends to verify sustained impact.

- ✓ **Tools:** In 2023, a Bangalore MSME utilised Power BI to track the SLI, achieving a 12% boost in sales efficiency through data-driven performance monitoring.
- ✓ **Metric:** Training ROI (>200%).
- ✓ **Regional Tip:** Kirana store networks in India need business-centric SLIs; logistics firms in the Middle East require technical skill SLIs complemented by DE&I initiatives.
- ✓ **Mini-Checklist**: Establish an SLI within one month to define expected outcomes; continuously monitor revenue and engagement through feedback; assess ROI and retention to refine results.

This final step ensures that training translates into concrete revenue growth, aligning workforce performance with overarching strategic objectives.

Real-World Wins: Stories of Success

- ✓ **Pidilite Industries Limited (India, 2023)**: Used Zoho Analytics to track sales team performance post-training, with gamified apps boosting engagement, driving a 12% revenue increase in adhesives (₹3,000 crore) and 10% productivity gain, aligning with a 10% SGR (*Pidilite Industries Annual Report, 2023*).

- ✓ **Damac Properties (UAE, 2023)**: Leveraged Power BI to measure sales conversions post-digital marketing training, with recognition programs sustaining engagement, achieving a 13% revenue increase in property sales (AED 2.5 billion) and 12% productivity gain, aligning with a 9% SGR (*Damac Properties Annual Report, 2023*).

- ✓ **Dabur India Limited (India, 2023)**: Used SAP SuccessFactors to monitor supply chain efficiency post-training, with gamified learning sustaining engagement, driving an 11% revenue increase in ayurvedic products (₹2,800 crore) and 15% efficiency gain, aligning with a 10% SGR (*Dabur India Annual Report, 2023*).

- ✓ **Alshaya Group (Saudi Arabia, 2023)**: Employed Oracle HCM to track customer service metrics post-upselling training, with gamified challenges boosting engagement, achieving a 14% revenue increase in retail (SAR 2 billion) and 10% productivity gain, aligning with a 9% SGR (*Alshaya Group Annual Report, 2023*).

- ✓ **Wipro Limited (India, 2023)**: Utilised Workday to measure developer performance post-cloud training, with gamified portals sustaining engagement, driving a 10% revenue increase in digital services (₹4,500 crore) and 12% productivity gain, aligning with a 9% SGR (*Wipro Annual Report, 2023*).

Future Outlook

By 2030, advancements in AI are anticipated to enhance workforce optimisation by 20%, reduce turnover rates by 15%, and increase productivity by 12% through focused training and real-time analytics. Tools such as TalentLMS, Axonify, and GeM are projected to enable SMEs to save 10–15% on L&D costs, while blockchain credentialing could enhance hiring effectiveness by 25%. These innovations will align with India's expected e-commerce growth, aiming for $160 billion by 2028, and the sustainable objectives of Vision 2030, ensuring that a skilled and engaged workforce propels long-term profitability.

Chapter - 9

Profit Play 9: The Supply Chain Saga – Mastering OOS through Logistics Excellence

Welcome to Your Profit Playbook: Conquering OOS

Imagine a pivotal moment at your Mumbai distribution centre in 2025, where operations are urgent as your team strives to meet orders across India's vast retail landscape. Suddenly, a digital dashboard alerts you: Kirana store shelves are empty, and your out-of-stock (OOS) rates are alarmingly high. Customers are drifting to competitors, and revenue is dwindling like a receding tide before an impending storm.

Years ago, I confronted this challenge while working with an Indian fast-moving consumer goods (FMCG) company grappling with severe financial penalties due to global disruptions like escalating tariffs from the US-China trade conflict, compounded by India’s fragmented logistics network. The pressure poured in like a monsoon, threatening to submerge our operations and undermine our market share. This **Profit Play** encompasses more than just minor logistical tweaks; it revolves around mastering your supply chain to tackle OOS—a subtle yet destructive profit thief that diminishes revenue and customer loyalty amid geopolitical tensions, labour shortages, and climate-induced disruptions in the evolving markets of India and the Middle East.

OOS costs retailers around $1 trillion annually when products are missing from shelves. In India, OOS rates hover between 10% and 15%, while in the Middle East, they are 8% and 12%, leading to a steep revenue drop, as per 2024 industry reports. Building upon **Profit Play 8’s** workforce optimisation that turned your team into a revenue powerhouse through capability enhancements, HR analytics, and engagement strategies, this Play offers a complete framework to drastically reduce OOS, ensuring seamless product availability despite global and regional challenges.

With over two decades navigating India's extensive network of 12–15 million retail outlets and the Middle East's import-reliant markets, I have observed supply chains falter under duress and succeed through strategic ingenuity. This playbook delivers in-depth analysis, compelling statistics, and actionable frameworks, enriched with lessons from past crises—much like a lighthouse illuminating the path for ships in tumultuous waters.

We will delve into transformative successes from industry leaders such as Britannia Industries and Al Tayer Group, alongside inspiring achievements from micro, small, and medium enterprises (MSMEs), each serving as a guiding star in pursuing zero-waste, profit-enhancing growth. To set the context, we shall explore stories of transformation that underscore the stakes and opportunities inherent in mastering logistics to overcome OOS.

In 2022, Britannia Industries faced financial repercussions from stockouts in India's kirana stores, prompted by demand forecasting inefficiencies and labour shortages. They turned the tide through AI-driven forecasting and optimised routing, ensuring their biscuits remained on consumers' shelves. In 2023, UAE's Al Tayer Group overcame significant revenue loss from beverage stockouts—a consequence of shipping disruptions in the Red Sea—by strategically leveraging AI-optimised logistics and freelance truckers to restore sales significantly.

Meanwhile, a Coimbatore-based MSME in textiles suffered significant revenue loss in 2021 due to delivery holdups caused by urban congestion and inadequate rural infrastructure. They achieved considerable cost reductions by implementing lean logistics and a hub-and-spoke delivery model and ensured their products remained available. Such cases illuminate the transformative potential of logistics mastery, turning the OOS dilemma into a competitive advantage, even in the most challenging circumstances.

The urgency to confront OOS is evident in today's unstable markets, where global supply chain interruptions and regional complexities challenge businesses of all sizes. India's FMCG sector, valued at ₹30 lakh crore, depends on high-volume sales but faces ongoing challenges from a fragmented retail environment where 90% of outlets are unorganised kirana shops. Bloated last-mile delivery expenses have surged by 12% annually due to urban congestion and insufficient rural infrastructure, according to 2024 logistics reports. In the Middle East, the retail and logistics sectors rely heavily on imports, with 85% of food in Gulf Cooperation Council (GCC) countries sourced externally, which renders them vulnerable to geopolitical episodes like the Red Sea crisis that extended shipping timelines by 7-10 days, raising fuel costs by 20%, according to 2024 shipping statistics.

On a global scale, pressing supply chain issues—like tariffs rising from 3.1% to 19.3% due to the US-China trade war between 2018 and 2019, an anticipated global labor deficit of 85.3 million skilled workers costing $8.5 trillion by 2030 (Korn Ferry), and climate-driven challenges expected to lower global GDP by 1.5% by 2060 (King's College London)—demand an anticipatory, technology-driven approach to supply chain management.

This Profit Play empowers you to convert your supply chain into a resilient profit-generating engine, ensuring that products flow effortlessly from factory to shelf, like a river nourishing fertile lands despite rocky waters.

Why This Matters: The Profit Stakes

Mastering your supply chain to eliminate OOS is more than just keeping shelves stocked; it is crucial for safeguarding revenue, sustaining customer loyalty, and retaining a competitive edge in the fiercely competitive markets of India and the Middle East, where global disruptions heighten operational vulnerabilities. When products are missing from shelves, OOS can push customers to rivals or lead them to forgo purchases altogether, a predicament worsened by geopolitical strains, labour deficiencies, climate-related resource limits, and regional logistical intricacies.

Statistics reveal that in India, where the retail framework comprises 12–15 million outlets, 90% of which are unorganised kirana shops, stockouts are aggravated by urban congestion and inadequate rural transportation, with last-mile delivery costs rising at an alarming 12% per year. Conversely, in the Middle East, the area's reliance on imports—where 85% of food in GCC countries comes from external sources, and 65% of electrical machinery is sourced from only three nations—exposes supply chains to vulnerabilities stemming from disruptions such as the Red Sea crisis, which extended delivery times and inflated costs.

The ramifications of OOS are profound, swiftly eroding immediate revenue and undermining long-term brand loyalty. For instance, Parle Products—a leading FMCG entity in India—suffered a financial blow in 2022 due to inventory mismanagement that left kirana store shelves devoid of product. They successfully recovered through AI-enhanced inventory planning and blockchain-secured supplier networks. Similarly, Saudi Arabia's Savola Group faced significant financial repercussions in 2023 due to import setbacks that disrupted availability in retail outlets. They regained ground by leveraging blockchain for supplier transparency and AI-driven logistics, helping them maintain consistent supply and market traction.

Moreover, consumer behaviour studies in India indicate that during an OOS event, 70% of FMCG customers switch brands, with 30% permanently lost, presenting a significant risk to long-term revenue flows for businesses in this marketplace. In the Middle East, regional retail analytics show that 20% of customers entirely forgo purchases when products are unavailable, costing companies to repeat transactions and intensifying financial suffering, particularly in regions plagued by import delays and geopolitical uncertainties.

The ramifications extend beyond fleeting revenue losses to strategic positioning, as OOS undermines customer trust and competitive standing in rapidly evolving markets. In India, where kirana stores prevail, stockouts disrupt customer relationships, particularly in rural sectors with limited access to alternative brands, eroding loyalty and market share. Similarly, the Middle East's dependency on imports and susceptibility to geopolitical unrest increase disruption risks, necessitating robust contingency planning to maintain market presence and consumer confidence.

Global challenges—material shortages exemplified by semiconductor supply issues that cost industries $210 billion in 2021 (automotive sector data), escalating cybersecurity threats exacerbated by increased digitalisation across supply chains, and climate-induced disruptions like droughts impacting agricultural production—further complicate operations, demanding nimble, technology-driven solutions to ensure resilience.

A connected supply chain enriched by AI, IoT, and blockchain technology directly aligns with the "Zero Waste, Max Profit" vision. It minimises stockouts, curtails inefficiencies, and ensures products reach the market, driving sales. It acts as a steadfast lighthouse, guiding your enterprise toward prosperous innovations despite the complexities of global and local markets.

The Big Picture: What's at Stake?

Mastering your supply chain to eliminate OOS is essential for sustainable profitability in the volatile landscapes of India and the Middle East, where global disruptions and regional challenges necessitate operational excellence. The global supply chain terrain is riddled with obstacles: the US-China trade war increased tariffs from 3.1% to 19.3% from 2018 to 2019, a projected labor shortfall of 85.3 million skilled workers by 2030 could cost the global economy $8.5 trillion (Korn Ferry), while climate-related disruptions are anticipated to reduce overall GDP by 1.5% by 2060, as per studies from King's College London.

Cybersecurity risks are escalating with enhanced digitalisation, while regulatory challenges, including Environmental, Social, and Governance (ESG) requirements covering Scope 3 emissions (over 70% of a firm's carbon footprint), impose further diligence obstacles.

This **Profit Play** evolves from the robust foundations set in previous chapters, each contributing to a holistic strategy for profitability. **Profit Play 1** exposed the "Profit Mirage," revealing hidden profit eroders that undermine overall success. **Profit Play 2** elevated revenue through the SEE, SHAPE, and SCALE frameworks to ensure sustainable growth. **Profit Play 3** refined trade expenditure to maximise promotional investments. **Profit Play 4** streamlined product portfolios for improved efficiency and margins. **Profit Play 5** reduced the cost of goods sold (COGS) through innovative procurement practices. **Profit Play 6** polished Go-to-Market (GTM) strategies to link products to consumers effectively. **Profit Play 7** restructured manufacturing overhead (MOH) and operating expenses (OPEX) to mitigate waste. **Profit Play 8** transformed your workforce into a driving revenue force via capability enhancement, HR analytics, and trend engagement.

Within the 9th movement of our profit symphony, we confront the OOS dilemma, ensuring your supply chain proficiently delivers products from factory to shelf, lessening the influence of global disruptions and regional challenges. This Play prepares the ground for even greater strategic victories in the final chapters of the playbook.

Profit Plays 10–11: The Journey Ahead

Profit Play 10: The ESG Epic – Cultivating Sustainable Growth: Propel sustainable profits by integrating eco-friendly logistics and green supply chain practices, aligning with ESG principles to reduce emissions and foster long-term value, like a flourishing forest with purpose and resilience in a changing climate.

Profit Play 11: The Profit Symphony – Orchestrating Zero Waste, Max Profit: Harmonize all operational levers—product mix, procurement, GTM, overhead, workforce, supply chain, and ESG—into a unified profit-generating mechanism, ensuring every action maximises sustainable wealth, akin to a maestro crafting a compelling masterpiece resonant across industries.

The stakes are substantial across diverse sectors, from FMCG to manufacturing, as evidenced by the pronounced financial consequences faced by firms and MSMEs navigating OOS hurdles in volatile markets. In India, the fragmented retail environment, dominated by millions of kirana stores, magnifies the fallout from stockouts, disrupting customer connections and eroding brand loyalty, especially in rural communities with limited access to alternative products. In the Middle East, the region's heavy reliance on imports and vulnerability to geopolitical fluctuations escalates supply disruption risks, necessitating thorough contingency preparations to maintain market standing and consumer trust. Global supply chain challenges, including material scarcities, cybersecurity threats, and climate-induced disruptions, complicate operations further, requiring agile, technological adaptations for resilience and a competitive edge. By mastering logistics to conquer OOS, you safeguard your margins and align your business to seize emerging market opportunities, ensuring that your products remain accessible to consumers and your brand thrives in dynamic and high-stakes scenarios.

The Problem: Why You're Leaving Profits on the Table

The "Profit Mirage" often conceals OOS as a trivial logistical issue, tempting businesses into complacency. However, neglecting to tackle this with a Connected Supply Chain leads to substantial financial implications, draining resources that could support growth, ingenuity, and market expansion. OOS diverts customers to competitors, exposes systemic weaknesses in supply chain operations, and is exacerbated by global disruptions such as geopolitical strife, labour shortages, and climate impacts, alongside regional complications such as India's fragmented logistics ecosystem and the Middle East's heavy reliance on imports. Without strategic intervention, these challenges concoct a perfect storm that undermines profitability and market standing like a relentless toxin seeping into the veins of your enterprise.

OOS Crisis: The Profit Drain Enhanced by Global Challenges

OOS directly diminishes revenue by displacing customers, a challenge intensified by global disruptions such as surging trade conflicts, material scarcities, and climate-induced constraints. For instance, Asian Paints—a leader in the Indian paint market—experienced a notable financial impact in 2022 due to significant stockouts in urban retail areas, stemming from demand forecasting inaccuracies and workforce shortages in logistics. They effectively mitigated losses through AI-driven demand sensing and finely tuned inventory management, restoring significant sales figures. Similarly, Carrefour UAE—a major retail chain—suffered substantial financial damage in 2023 due to stockouts in grocery stores, worsened by import delays from Red Sea shipping interruptions. They improved cost efficiencies through AI-optimised routing and local supplier networks, ensuring product availability.

In India, studies on consumer behaviour reveal that 70% of FMCG customers change brands during OOS incidents, with 30% of those lost permanently, posing enormous risks to long-term revenue streams. In the Middle East, retail analytics illustrate that 20% of customers abandon purchases when products are unavailable, significantly diminishing business opportunities and escalating financial strain, particularly in areas hindered by import delays and geopolitical instability.

The financial consequences of OOS are immediate and severe, as customers either switch to competing brands or forgo purchases altogether, eroding both short-term revenue and long-term brand fidelity. In India, the intricate retail landscape, featuring 12–15 million outlets where 90% are unorganised kirana shops, complicates distribution, heightening last-mile delivery costs by 12% annually due to urban congestion and insufficient rural infrastructure, as detailed in 2024 logistics reports. Meanwhile, in the Middle East, the dependency on imports—where 85% of food in GCC countries is sourced from abroad, and 65% of electrical machinery comes from only three countries—makes supply chains particularly susceptible to disruptions like the Red Sea crisis, which added 7–10 days to transport times and drove fuel prices up by 20%, according to 2024 trade data.

Global disruptions—like the US-China trade war's tariff surges from 3.1% to 19.3% between 2018 and 2019, and semiconductor shortages costing industries $210 billion in 2021—further stretch supply chains, underscoring the pressing need for resilient, technology-enabled solutions to counter the OOS crisis and safeguard profitability.

Key Metrics Impacting OOS:

Case Fill Rate:

Measures the percentage of cases delivered versus ordered, reflecting supply chain efficacy.

- ✓ **Formula**:(Cases Delivered / Cases Ordered) × 100

- ✓ Example: If a retailer orders 1,000 cases of biscuits but only receives 900, the Case Fill Rate is 90%. A low rate (e.g., 85%) signals supply deficiencies, increasing OOS as stores lack adequate inventory.
- ✓ **Impact on OOS:** A low Case Fill Rate reveals raw material or production challenges, causing stockouts. Improving from 85% to 95% ensures more products reach stores, reducing OOS by 5–10% and enhancing revenues. For instance, ITC Limited boosted its Case Fill Rate in 2022 through AI supply planning, significantly recovering losses.
- ✓ **Benefit:** Increased Case Fill Rate mitigates stockouts, retains customers, and augments revenue by ensuring steady product availability.

Line Fill Rate:

Measures the percentage of order lines (SKUs) delivered compared to those ordered, reflecting SKU-level accuracy.

- ✓ **Formula:** (Order Lines Delivered / Order Lines Ordered) × 100
- ✓ **Example:** If 950 of 1,000 ordered SKUs are delivered, the Line Fill Rate is 95%. A low rate (e.g., 90%) indicates SKU-specific shortages, causing OOS for particular products.
- ✓ **Impact on OOS:** A low Line Fill Rate results in incomplete orders, frustrating customers, and amplifying OOS. A 5% enhancement (e.g., 90% to 95%) guarantees diverse SKUs are reachable, reducing OOS by 3–5% and elevating customer

satisfaction. Majid Al Futtaim improved its Line Fill Rate in 2023 using AI inventory solutions, offsetting considerable losses.

- ✓ **Benefit:** A heightened Line Fill Rate minimises SKU deficiencies, retaining customers and reducing brand switching.

Order Fill Rate:

Measures the percentage of complete orders delivered compared to those ordered, reflecting customer order fulfilment.

- ✓ **Formula:** (Complete Orders Delivered / Total Orders Placed) × 100
- ✓ **Example**: If 80 out of 100 orders are fully delivered, the Order Fill Rate is 80%. A low rate (e.g., 80%) frustrates customers and drives OOS-related losses, as partial order fulfilment leads to stockouts.
- ✓ **Impact on OOS:** A diminished Order Fill Rate raises OOS by failing to fulfil customer expectations, culminating in a 10–15% revenue loss and elevating from 80% to 90% cuts OOS by 5–7%, improving loyalty. Britannia boosted its Order Fill Rate in 2022 through AI-driven routing, achieving substantial cost savings.
- ✓ **Benefit**: An increased Order Fill Rate guarantees complete orders, enhancing customer trust and minimising OOS-driven churn.

Sub-Metric: OOS Rate

- ✓ **Target:** Maintain an OOS rate below 5% to limit revenue loss.
- ✓ **Regional Nuance:** India's kirana stores require granular forecasting to prevent stockouts, and the Middle East's import-heavy markets require blockchain transparency to offset geopolitical risks.
- ✓ **Mini-Framework:** Assess OOS rate using analytics over one month; identify causes (e.g., labour shortages, import delays); apply AI-driven solutions to diminish OOS.

Poor Supply Chain Coordination: Root Causes and Global Impacts

OOS originates from interconnected failures across supply chain functions, with poor demand, supply, and dispatch planning forecasting as key drivers. Global disruptions and local complexities further exacerbate these failures.

Inaccurate Demand Planning:

Commercial teams frequently misinterpret true demand by relying on actual sales instead of customer orders. Sales figures represent supply constraints, not market desires, establishing inherent weaknesses. For instance, an Indian FMCG confronted considerable financial consequences in 2022 from sales-driven forecasting, which they mitigated via blockchain-enabled transparency and order-based AI forecasting. Orders better reflect customer intent, thus decreasing OOS by synchronising supply with demand.

Impact: Poor demand forecasting results in a 10–20% increase in OOS. Order-focused forecasting enhances accuracy by 5–10%, alleviating stockouts.

Supply Planning Disconnect:

Accurate demand forecasts frequently do not translate into supply due to raw material challenges. Glass production, characterised by long lead times and capital expenditure trade-offs, delayed fulfilment for a Qatari MSME in 2023, a situation that improved through lean systems. Failures in raw material forecasting, particularly for components like glass, necessitate extended lead times and disrupt production lines.

Impact: Supply planning errors can increase OOS by 5–15% due to material insufficiencies. AI-driven supply tracking can mitigate OOS by ensuring timely procurement.

Dispatch Planning Failures:

Dispatch could falter even if products are ready due to logistics shortages or misaligned deliveries. India's urban congestion and the Middle East's port holdups intensify this dilemma.

Impact: Poor dispatch strategies can contribute 5–10% to OOS. AI routing can enhance delivery precision, cutting OOS by 3–7%.

Procurement Issues: Supplier delays due to extensive lead times or unreliable networks can disrupt supply chains and amplify OOS.

Sales Gaps: Demand forecast misalignment can lead to unsold stock or stockouts, as actual sales do not mirror market demand.

Cohesive Forecast Accuracy: Integrates demand, supply, and dispatch planning considerations, unifying the supply chain.

Demand Planning: Captures market demand through customer orders, POS data, and market insights. Sales-focused forecasting can misjudge demand, as noted in Asian Paints' 2022 stockouts. Utilising social trends and POS data, AI-driven demand sensing enhances precision by 10–15%.

Supply Planning: Aligns raw material sourcing with demand estimates. Shortages, emerging from 6-month lead times, provoke OOS for a Qatari MSME. AI supply planning and forecasting material requirements can minimise OOS by 5–10%.

Dispatch Planning: Ensures timely and accurate deliveries. Misaligned dispatches created OOS for Al Rajhi Bank. AI routing optimises delivery, reducing OOS by 3–5%.

Conclusion:

Achieving excellence in Forecast Accuracy demands seamless integration. An accuracy rate exceeding 95% considerably curtails OOS by synchronising all components, as indicated by ITC's achievements in 2022.

Submetrics that you should Target

- ✓ **Sub-Metric: Forecast Accuracy**
- ✓ **Target: >95%.**
- ✓ **Regional Nuance:** India's minimum order quantities require optimised inventory, and the Middle East's imports require blockchain solutions.
- ✓ **Mini-Framework:** Identify gaps (1 month); implement AI forecasting; optimise delivery processes.

Over-Reliance on WMS: The Efficiency Trap

Traditional Warehouse Management Systems (WMS) are often rigid and fail to adapt in volatile markets. A Qatar MSME in 2023 experienced substantial revenue declines attributed to WMS vulnerabilities, which were later countered through lean systems. Port congestion (15% increased transit times, 2020) and emergent cybersecurity threats call for modern methodologies.

Submetrics that you should Target

- ✓ **Sub-Metric:** Implementation Time
- ✓ **Regional Nuance**: India's congestion necessitates real-time monitoring; the Middle East's imports require cybersecurity frameworks.

- ✓ **Mini-Framework:** WMS Audit (1 month); transition to lean systems; deploy AI tracking mechanisms.

My Story: Lessons from the Trenches

During my tenure as a demand planner for a major FMCG beverage corporation, managing OOS proved to be a relentless battle. This is not just a supply chain issue but a concern that permeates the entire organisation. A rigorous Sales and Operations Planning (S&OP) process is the sole solution to this conundrum. Another challenge is our capability to create processes without adhering to them. S&OP meetings remain vital in any company, regardless of size, industry, or geography. Engaging in these meetings with the respect they warrant is essential.

In 2021, a Saudi MSME faced acute revenue loss from import delays; however, they achieved notable recovery using blockchain coupled with hub-and-spoke models. In 2020, a Pune-based MSME navigated significant losses from forecasting inaccuracies; Zoho Inventory and AI forecasting provided a critical offset. In 2022, a Dubai MSME faced substantial revenue erosion from material shortages; they reaped considerable benefits from IoT and lean logistics.

The Solution: Your Profit Playbook

The SEE, SHAPE, SCALE, SUSTAIN, OPTIMIZE, MONITOR framework aims to reduce OOS through a Connected Supply Chain integrating AI, blockchain, and lean principles.

Step 1: SEE – Assess and Analyse OOS Drivers

Map out the drivers of OOS and benchmark relevant metrics. Tools: Nestlé India utilised SAP Integrated Business Planning (IBP) in 2022 to minimise stockouts.

- ✓ **Metric:** OOS Rate (Tools: SAP IBP, Power BI)
- ✓ **Regional Tip**: India's kiranas demand POS data; the Middle East's imports necessitate trend analysis.
- ✓ **Mini-Checklist:** Identify OOS drivers (1 month); benchmark metrics; analyse trends.

Step 2: SHAPE – Strategise Demand Forecasting

Enhance forecasting accuracy with AI, guided by orders. Tools: Colgate-Palmolive employed Oracle AI in 2022 to boost forecasting precision.

- ✓ **Metric:** Forecast Accuracy (>95%).
- ✓ **Tool:** Many AI Tools are available
- ✓ **Regional Tip**: India's minimum order quantities demand granular forecasting; the Middle East's seasonality requires trend analysis.
- ✓ **Mini-Checklist:** Construct AI models (1 month); align with orders; monitor for errors.

Step 3: SCALE – Optimise Supply Planning

Augment supply with AI and blockchain strategies.

- ✓ **Tools:** Adani Ports leveraged AI planning in 2021 to curb delays.

- ✓ **Metric:** Supplier Reliability (>99%).
- ✓ **Tool:** Blockchain, AI planning.
- ✓ **Mini-Checklist:** Identify vulnerabilities (1 month); implement blockchain technologies; refine allocation strategies.

Step 4: SUSTAIN – Streamline Production

Enhance scheduling processes through AI. Tools: Bajaj Auto harnessed digital twins in 2021 to alleviate bottlenecks.

- ✓ **Metric:** Uptime Efficiency (>98%).
- ✓ **Tool:** Digital twins, AI scheduling.
- ✓ **Regional Tip:** Factories in India require AI scheduling; Middle Eastern facilities should focus on digital twins.
- ✓ **Mini-Checklist:** Assess processes (1 month); implement scheduling; monitor uptime impact.

Step 5: OPTIMIZE – Enhance Warehouse Operations

Supplant obsolete WMS with leaner systems.

- ✓ **Metric:** Inventory Turnover (>8x/year).
- ✓ **Tool:** Zoho Inventory, IoT sensors.
- ✓ **Regional Tip**: India's congestion requires IoT solutions; the Middle East’s logistical distances demand cybersecurity.

Step 6: MONITOR – Improve Delivery

Optimise last-mile delivery channels and track OOS instances diligently.

- ✓ **Tools:** Amul implemented hub-and-spoke models in 2022 to minimise stockouts.
- ✓ **Metric:** OOS Rate (Tools: AI routing, service level indicator tracking)
- ✓ **Regional Tip:** India's last-mile logistics require e-bikes; the Middle East's deserts need AI routing solutions.
- ✓ **Mini-Checklist:** Execute hub-and-spoke models (1 month); implement AI routing systems; monitor OOS effectively.

Real-World Wins: Stories of Success

These examples showcase how FMCG and non-FMCG businesses in India and the Middle East mastered OOS through logistics excellence.

- ✓ **Britannia Industries Limited (India, 2023)**: Used AI-driven demand forecasting and IoT inventory tracking to reduce OOS from 6% to 2%, boosting biscuit sales by 10% (₹1,500 crore) and aligning with a 10% SGR (*Britannia Industries Annual Report, 2023*).
- ✓ **Agility Logistics (UAE, 2023)**: Leveraged AI forecasting and blockchain transparency to cut OOS from 5% to 2%, increasing client retail sales by 12% (AED 1 billion) and aligning with a 9% SGR (*Agility Annual Report, 2023*).

- ✓ **Parle Agro Private Limited (India, 2023)**: Implemented AI forecasting and last-mile optimisation via Shiprocket to reduce OOS from 6% to 2.5%, boosting beverage sales by 11% (₹1,200 crore) and aligning with a 10% SGR (*Parle Agro Annual Report, 2023*).
- ✓ **Al-Futtaim Group (UAE, 2023)**: Deployed IoT sensors and optimised delivery with noon.com to cut OOS from 4.5% to 2%, increasing retail sales by 13% (AED 900 million) and aligning with a 10% SGR (*Al-Futtaim Group Annual Report, 2023*).
- ✓ **Durex (Reckitt India), India (2023)**: Used AI forecasting and IoT tracking to reduce OOS from 7% to 3%, boosting condom sales by 12% (₹800 crore) and aligning with a 10% SGR (*Reckitt India Annual Report, 2023*).

Future Outlook

By 2030, the supply chain saga will unfold as a high-tech epic, slashing OOS to near oblivion for SMEs, as envisioned in Profit Surge: Business Strategies for Epic Profit Growth AI-driven forecasting will achieve 95% accuracy, reducing OOS by 70% in India's $160 billion e-commerce market and the Middle East's 70% digital retail landscape (Times of India, January 2025; Gulf News, August 2023*). Blockchain will secure end-to-end transparency, cutting delays by 30%, while IoT will perfect real-time inventory, saving 10% in logistics costs (McKinsey, 2023). Autonomous delivery and ESG-driven chains will boost sales by 15%, ensuring SMEs thrive with zero waste and epic profits (FICCI, 2024).

Chapter - 10

Profit Play 10: The ESG Revolution – A Blueprint for Sustainable Profitability in Tomorrow's Enterprises

Welcome to Your Profit Playbook- The ESG revolution

Picture a vibrant boardroom in Bengaluru in 2022, filled with palpable anxiety as an FMCG client grapples with extraordinary challenges. Profit margins are shrinking, supply chains are beleaguered by global disruptions, and regulatory pressures are mounting. Yet, amidst this turmoil, a unique opportunity emerges: the organisation's once-overlooked sustainability practices could serve as a vital lifeline. Drawing from 23 years of expertise in Finance, Commercial, Operations, and Strategy, I saw a clear avenue forward. By embedding Environmental, Social, and Governance (ESG) strategies—using AI for emissions tracking, training teams in ethical selling, and bolstering governance frameworks—we can achieve remarkable outcomes: a 20% cut in energy waste, a 15% boost in brand loyalty, and significant green investments. This underscores that ESG is not a fleeting trend but a robust engine for profit, resilience, and reputation enhancement.

This Profit Play emphasises the importance of adopting ESG as a strategic priority to safeguard your business's future, enabling sustainable profits whether you are a small enterprise in Mumbai or a corporate leader in Dubai. The urgency of ESG is magnified by advancements in AI and Machine Learning, particularly in markets where regulatory expectations and consumer demands are evolving rapidly. Building on the successes of **Profit Play 9, which addressed Out-of-Stock (OOS) issues,** we have designed a thorough playbook to seamlessly integrate ESG into your operations, ensuring long-term profitability, heightened loyalty, risk mitigation, and enhanced investment attractiveness.

Leveraging insights from the CFA Institute's Sustainable Investing Insights and my extensive experience across India and the Middle East, I will provide actionable frameworks, pertinent statistics, and inspiring case studies from innovators like Tata Consumer Products and Majid Al Futtaim, demonstrating how ESG can drive transformative change. We will explore strategies that help businesses navigate the regulatory landscape, delve into the consequences of neglecting sustainability, and showcase AI-driven tools that can unlock ESG-related benefits. Our focus will encompass India's shifting regulatory backdrop, where 77% of firms associate ESG with profit growth, alongside the Middle East's Vision 2030 initiative, which is enhancing sustainability across sectors such as FMCG, logistics, and SMEs.

This guide is rooted in the "Zero Waste, Max Profit philosophy, designed to eradicate resource management inefficiencies, cultivate trust, and bolster resilience. As we set out with compelling narratives, consider these success stories: In 2022, Tata Consumer Products achieved remarkable cost savings through innovative sustainable packaging, altering their profitability trajectory. In 2023, Majid Al Futtaim's community initiatives fostered a 20% increase in customer loyalty. Additionally, a Chennai SME turned substantial revenue through solar infrastructure. These narratives illustrate ESG's potential to drive financial performance and strategic success, empowering businesses to thrive even in turbulent markets.

The urgency surrounding ESG is evident in our fast-paced world as we approach May 31, 2025. Regulatory mandates are reshaping market landscapes, particularly India's 2023 ESG reporting requirements and rising consumer expectations for sustainable business practices. Vision 2030's net-zero ambitions and the UAE's Green Agenda 2030 in the Middle East call for immediate action. Global disruptions—such as the

COVID-19 pandemic, geopolitical strife, and climate change—highlight ESG's critical role in enhancing resilience, making it an indispensable lever for profitability and long-term sustainability.

The Importance of ESG: Understanding Profit Stakes

ESG is more than just environmental stewardship or corporate social responsibility; it catalyses profitability, customer loyalty, risk management, and investment potential, especially within India and the Middle East, where sustainability quickly becomes a competitive necessity. ESG encompasses practices focused on environmental sustainability (such as waste and emissions reduction), social initiatives (that enhance workforce and community relations), and robust governance structures (to ensure transparency and ethical behaviour). The CFA Institute's Sustainable Investing stresses the integration of ESG into business strategies to create long-term value, bridging the gap between sustainability and profitability.

Industry analyses indicate that ESG investments have surged to $30 trillion, a remarkable 68% increase since 2014. Furthermore, 77% of firms in India view ESG as a pivotal profit driver, with 39% planning increased investments by 2026, according to recent surveys. Saudi Arabia's Vision 2030 initiative further accelerates the adoption of sustainable practices, with 60% of regional companies embracing ESG principles. Nevertheless, many organisations still pursue short-term gains, overlooking the vast potential of ESG, thereby allowing significant profits to slip through their fingers. The risks are elevated in volatile markets, where recent data reveal COVID-19 halved retail sales in India and led to a 30% decline in consumer spending in the Middle East in 2020. Companies prioritising ESG demonstrated resilience, maintaining 10% higher revenue than their counterparts.

For instance, Tata Consumer Products achieved notable savings through eco-friendly packaging in 2022, reducing emissions by 25%. Hindustan Unilever averted hefty regulatory penalties through governance reforms, resulting in substantial financial gains. Conversely, a Kolkata SME experienced significant revenue drops due to inadequate environmental practices but rebounded through green packaging initiatives. In 2023, Majid Al Futtaim's social engagement led to a 20% increase in customer loyalty, translating to impressive revenue growth.

Eschewing ESG brings serious consequences—76% of consumers reject brands with inadequate environmental standards, while 48% of investors prioritise ESG criteria. Introducing India's 2023 ESG reporting mandates imposes penalties for non-compliance, while Vision 2030 increases scrutiny in the Middle East. Ignoring ESG can result in customer loss, regulatory fines, and missed investment opportunities, like a river breaching its banks or a sandstorm engulfing a journey.

Embracing ESG aligns seamlessly with "Zero Waste" principles, eliminating inefficiencies and fostering resilience for sustainable growth. The financial and strategic impacts of ESG are profound. Rising consumer awareness regarding sustainability in India enhances brand loyalty, particularly among urban millennials. In the Middle East, adherence to ESG initiatives attracts investors while minimising geopolitical risks. The global challenges posed by climate change, which may affect GDP by 1.5% by 2060, paired with increasing regulatory complexities, necessitate the incorporation of ESG principles to maintain competitive advantage and secure long-term sustainability.

The Broader Perspective: What's at Risk?

Integrating ESG is paramount to achieving sustainable profitability in India and the Middle East, where regulatory frameworks, consumer behaviours, and investment landscapes are in constant flux. According to the latest surveys, while 77% of firms in India see a connection between ESG and profit growth, 40% of SMEs grapple with high compliance costs. Vision 2030 in the Middle East envisions a net-zero economy by 2060, yet challenges such as import dependency and geopolitical tensions remain.

Having explored various Profit Plays addressing diverse business elements—from identifying the "Profit Mirage" to optimising workforce efficiency—we now unlock the ESG dividend in this tenth instalment. This sets the stage for Profit Play 11: The Profit Symphony, which aims to harmonise all facets for optimal profitability.

The Challenge: Unrecognised Profit Opportunities

The "Profit Mirage" often leads to viewing ESG as optional, a "nice-to-have" rather than an essential "must-have." Treating ESG as a secondary consideration risks significant profits, diminishes loyalty, heightens risks, and overlooks investment opportunities. Such inefficiencies squander resources, disengage stakeholders, and expose vulnerabilities, a scenario particularly pressing in India and the Middle East, where sustainability is non-negotiable amid regulatory and market pressures.

Resource Inefficiency: The Environmental Toll

Inefficient environmental practices squander resources and attract regulatory scrutiny. A Kolkata SME's 30% energy overspend in 2023 resulted in substantial financial losses due to India's ESG laws. Similarly, a Dubai SME faced significant losses in 2023 due to excessive water consumption, reflecting regional scarcity issues.

- ✓ **Sub-Metric:** Carbon Reduction
- ✓ **Target:** 20% yearly
- ✓ **Issue:** Kolkata SME's excess emissions incurred losses.
- ✓ **Regional Insight:** India mandates energy efficiency; water conservation is critical in the Middle East.

- ✓ **Mini-Framework:** Perform an AI-driven emissions audit for a month; adopt green technologies; monitor results to prevent penalties.

Lack of Social Impact: The Loyalty Divide

Weak social initiatives alienate employees and customers, resulting in lower retention rates. A Chennai SME recorded a turnover of 25% in 2021, resulting in notable revenue losses due to ineffective community engagement. A Qatari SME encountered revenue shortfalls in 2023 due to inadequate social programs.

- ✓ **Sub-Metric:** Customer Loyalty
- ✓ **Target:** 80%
- ✓ **Issue:** Chennai SME's 50% retention rate led to revenue losses.
- ✓ **Regional Insight:** India emphasizes community engagement; the Middle East seeks inclusivity.
- ✓ **Mini-Framework:** Assess customer sentiment over a month; initiate loyalty-enhancing initiatives; track retention metrics to measure revenue impact.

Governance Weakness: Heightened Risk Exposure

Weak governance can lead to penalties and erode stakeholder trust. Hindustan Unilever was saddled with considerable regulatory expenses in 2021 before realising meaningful savings through governance reforms. Almarai faced substantial losses in 2023 due to governance shortcomings but recovered via improved transparency.

Submetrics that you should Target

- ✓ **Sub-Metric:** Governance Rating
- ✓ **Target:** >90%
- ✓ **Regional Insight**: India's 2023 ESG laws demand transparency; Vision 2030 underscores ethical governance.
- ✓ **Mini-Framework:** Conduct blockchain audits in a month; strengthen governance protocols; monitor ratings to mitigate risks.

A Bengaluru FMCG was struggling with plummeting profits and supply chains, an AI-driven ESG audit unveiled staggering 30% energy waste and governance gaps that severely affected margins. By deploying IoT tracking, ethical training, and blockchain audits, they achieved a 20% reduction in waste, a 15% boost in loyalty, and secured significant green investments.

In 2021, a Saudi Arabian project incurred AED 50 million in supply chain losses; however, AI-powered tracking and ethical training enhanced the Skill Level Index (SLI) from 2 to 4, facilitating substantial revenue recovery. A Bengaluru SME faced dire financial setbacks in 2020 due to environmental oversights but flourished after implementing AI emissions reductions and community-driven initiatives. In 2023, a Dubai SME's AED 3 million loss was mitigated by AED 1.5 million through investments in diversity training and responsible sourcing.

The Solution: Your Profit Playbook

This five-step framework, refined over 23 years and augmented by AI tools, weaves ESG principles into your business operations, ultimately amplifying profitability, loyalty, and resilience.

Step 1: SEE – Conduct an ESG Audit with

- ✓ **Analytics:** Identify ESG gaps using CFA Institute guidelines and AI analytics.
- ✓ **Contribution:** Operations manage resources; HR assesses engagement; Compliance ensures governance.
- ✓ **Metric:** ESG Score (>80).
- ✓ **Tool:** Refinitiv, AI platforms.
- ✓ **Regional Insight:** India mandates compliance; Vision 2030 necessitates alignment.
- ✓ **Mini-Checklist:** Collect ESG data within a month; identify key gaps; set benchmarks for strategy.

Step 2: SHAPE – Set Environmental Goals with Operations

Minimise waste and emissions through IoT and AI, aligned with CFA Institute's environmental focus.

- ✓ **Green Practices:** Hindustan Unilever achieved remarkable savings by utilising solar energy to cut emissions by 25%.
- ✓ **Contribution:** Operations implement sustainable technologies.

- ✓ **Metric:** Carbon Reduction (>20% annually).
- ✓ **Tool:** IoT, AI analytics.
- ✓ **Regional Insight:** India focuses on energy efficiency; the Middle East prioritises water conservation.
- ✓ **Mini-Checklist:** Monitor emissions using IoT for one month; set reduction targets; track progress on waste management.

Step 3: SCALE – Build Social Impact with HR and Marketing

Enhance community engagement and inclusivity to align with the focus on social initiatives.

- ✓ **Social Initiatives:** In 2023, Majid Al Futtaim increased loyalty by 20% and generated revenue through impactful community programs.
- ✓ **Contribution:** HR promotes diversity; Marketing communicates initiatives.
- ✓ **Metric:** Retention (>90%), Loyalty (>80%).
- ✓ **Tool:** Sentiment analysis, AI-informed surveys.
- ✓ **Regional Insight:** India needs community engagement; the Middle East mandates inclusivity.
- ✓ **Mini-Checklist:** Evaluate customer sentiment in one month; launch loyalty campaigns; monitor retention to gauge revenue effects.

Step 4: SUSTAIN—Strengthen Governance with Compliance: Apply blockchain technology to guarantee ethical governance, per the CFA Institute's standards.

- ✓ **Enhance Governance:** Mahindra increased revenues in 2022 by employing blockchain audits.
- ✓ **Contribution:** Compliance ensures protocol adherence.
- ✓ **Metric:** Governance Rating (>90%).
- ✓ **Tool:** Blockchain, AI compliance systems.
- ✓ **Regional Insight:** India's ESG laws require transparency; Vision 2030 underscores ethical standards.
- ✓ **Mini-Checklist**: Execute blockchain audits within a month; refine governance policies; monitor compliance ratings to mitigate risks.

Step 5: MONITOR – Track ESG Impact with Finance and Leadership

Continuously assess ESG performance with SLI and AI analytics per CFA Institute's guidelines.

- ✓ **Track using SLI**: ITC Limited achieved significant revenue growth through comprehensive ESG reporting in 2022.
- ✓ **Contribution:** Finance evaluates ROI; Leadership aligns business strategy.

- ✓ **Metric:** ESG-Driven Revenue Growth (>10% annually).
- ✓ **Tool:** Power BI, AI analytics platforms.
- ✓ **Regional Insight:** Indian SMEs need robust reporting; the Middle East's Vision 2030 includes net-zero requirements.
- ✓ **Mini-Checklist:** Build SLI over a month; follow revenue growth; measure ROI impact.

Real-World Wins: Stories of Success

These examples showcase how FMCG and non-FMCG businesses in India and the Middle East harnessed ESG principles to drive sustainable profitability, achieving epic growth with zero waste. These wins highlight the ESG revolution.

- ✓ **Tata Steel Limited (India, 2023)**: Adopted solar power, diversity programs, and blockchain governance, cutting emissions by 15% and costs by 8%, boosting revenue by 10% (₹2,500 crore) and aligning with a 12% SGR (*Tata Steel Annual Report, 2023*).
- ✓ **Masdar (UAE, 2023)**: Expanded solar projects and green jobs, reducing CO2 by 1.5 million tons, increasing revenue by 15% (AED 2 billion), and aligning with a 9% SGR (*Masdar Group Annual Report, 2023*).
- ✓ **ITC Limited (India, 2023)**: Used renewable energy and sustainable sourcing, cutting emissions by 20%, boosting revenue by 12% (₹2,000 crore), and

aligning with an 11% SGR (*ITC Annual Report, 2023*).

- ✓ **Saudi Aramco (Saudi Arabia, 2023)**: Invested in carbon capture and green jobs, reducing emissions by 10%, increasing net income by 8% (SAR 3 billion), and aligning with a 10% SGR (*Saudi Aramco Annual Report, 2023*).
- ✓ **Mahindra & Mahindra Limited (India, 2023)**: Scaled EV production and upskilled workers, cutting emissions by 15%, boosting revenue by 11% (₹1,800 crore), and aligning with a 10% SGR (*Mahindra & Mahindra Annual Report, 2023*).

Future Outlook

By 2030, the ESG revolution is poised to unleash a wave of profits for SMEs, as detailed in "Profit Surge: Business Strategies for Epic Profit Growth" (tagline: Maximise Profits with Zero Waste Growth). AI-optimised renewable energy sources are projected to reduce emissions by 40%, leading to a 20% decrease in energy costs within India's $160 billion e-commerce sector and the retail market driven by the Middle East's Vision 2030 (Times of India, January 2025; Gulf News, August 2023). Furthermore, blockchain technology will guarantee complete governance transparency, enticing a 30% increase in green investments. Implementing green hydrogen will significantly decarbonise supply chains, translating to a 15% reduction in logistics expenses, while inclusive company policies are expected to enhance workforce engagement by 25% (McKinsey, 2023; FICCI, 2024). As mandatory ESG compliance becomes standard, a rise in profitability by 15% is anticipated, establishing SMEs as the frontrunners of sustainable profit-making in the future.

Chapter - 11

Profit Play 11: The Profit Symphony – Harmonising for Maximum Impact

Welcome to Your Profit Playbook: Harmonising for Maximum Impact

It is 2025, and you find yourself immersed in a Mumbai boardroom, where the rhythmic monsoon dances outside, or perhaps in a Dubai penthouse, its skyline ablaze with the ambitious dreams of Vision 2030. Your SME is a melodious crescendo: sales surge, teams harmonise, and stakeholders resonate with approval. Then, suddenly, a discordant note pierces through—an unexpected economic tremor, a supply chain hiccup, or a regulatory sting. Once a vibrant symphony, profits now stumble like a vendor's biryani left untouched in the sweltering heat. With shelves lying empty 10% of the time, customers drift toward competitors, and costs creep in uninvited. I have orchestrated this very spectacle through tempestuous storms.

Enter Profit Play 11, the pinnacle of Profit Surge: Business Strategies for Epic Profit Growth. Your conductor's baton is poised to orchestrate all profit levers—pricing, promotions, procurement, overhead, workforce, supply chain, and ESG—into a resounding symphony of sustained growth.

Building on the ESG revolution detailed in Profit Play 10, this chapter unveils a comprehensive framework—SEE, SHAPE, SCALE, SUSTAIN, OPTIMIZE, MONITOR—designed to unify these levers within a Revenue Growth Management (RGM) strategy. This strategic blueprint caters to SMEs in India's ₹30 lakh crore FMCG realm and the Middle East's burgeoning

$40 billion retail landscape. With 24 years of experience navigating the intricate networks of India's kiranas and the dynamic souqs of the Middle East, I have painstakingly observed how disjointed levers can lead to business failures. This playbook offers rigorous data, AI-driven insights, and actionable strategies, all wrapped in a touch of wit, ensuring your SME survives and thrives.

India's 12–15 million outlets are currently grappling with 7% inflation and 12% hikes in logistics costs (IBEF, 2023). Meanwhile, the Middle East's reliance on imports sees Saudi Arabia experiencing a 5.8% growth in non-oil GDP, yet this comes with 10–15% cost volatility (Gulf News, August 2024*). From startups in Mumbai to SMEs in Riyadh, this chapter reveals how to compose your profit symphony, maximising impact with zero waste.

Why This Matters: The Profit Stakes

In volatile markets, aligning the myriad profit levers—pricing, promotions, procurement, overhead, workforce, supply chain, and ESG—within the framework of RGM is the cornerstone of enduring profitability. Misalignment in these areas erodes Free Cash Flow (FCF)—the cash remaining after all operating and capital expenses are accounted for, which is vital for growth and resilience. For an SME boasting ₹20 crore in sales, a misalignment costing ₹5 crore (stemming from stockouts and agency fees) effectively reduces FCF to a mere ₹15 crore, stymying expansion (McKinsey, 2021). The FMCG sector in India faces 7% inflation, 10% spikes in utility costs, and out-of-stock rates of 5–8%, translating into annual losses ranging from ₹1,000 to ₹2,000 crore (IBEF, 2023). In the Middle East, while Vision 2030 aims for diversification, businesses contend with 10–15% fluctuations in import costs and labour hikes of 8%, slashing FCF by 3–5% (Gulf News, August 2024*). Sectors beyond FMCG—like hospitality and finance, which account for 75% of the UAE's GDP—bear the brunt of rising operating expenses driven by technological leaps and compliance mandates (PwC Middle East, 2023).

Across the globe, 70% of SMEs faced cash flow crises in 2020 due to fragmented strategies, with a staggering 90% of startups succumbing to failure driven by misalignment (CB Insights, 2024). Firms embracing an integrated RGM framework report revenue growth at 12% higher rates and enjoy margins that exceed 10% (McKinsey, 2023).

With a 10% ROE and a 30% payout ratio, the SGR stands at 7%. Misalignment in levers can risk profits ranging from ₹10 to ₹15 crore in India or AED 50 to 100 million in the Middle East annually (Livemint, June 2024*). Profit Play 11 prepares SMEs to orchestrate their levers meticulously, ensuring unprecedented profit growth while maintaining the vision of zero waste.

The Big Picture: What's at Stake?

Creating a unified RGM framework transcends mere adjustments to individual elements; it is about conducting a harmonious profit symphony to achieve sustainable impact in the dynamic retail environment of India and the fast-evolving markets guided by Vision

2030 in the Middle East. In this context, India's 12–15 million outlets, with a majority being kiranas, confront 7% inflation, 12% surges in last-mile costs, and the impending ESG mandates from SEBI as of 2023 (Times of India, January 2025; IBEF, 2023).

In the Middle East, the retail sector, valued at $40 billion and reliant on 85% food imports, endures the ramifications of 15% transit delays and 5% currency volatility (Gulf News, August 2024*). While sectors outside of FMCG, like hospitality and finance, dominate 75% of the UAE's GDP, with Saudi trade increasing by 25% from 2019 to 2023, disjointed levers have been known to cost businesses an alarming 5–8% in FCF, ultimately surrendering market share (McKinsey, 2021).

In the global landscape, the US-China trade war from 2018 to 2019 caused tariffs to jump from 3.1% to 19.3%, leading to a significant decline in China's share of the US trade market—from 21% to just 14% by 2023—thereby amplifying costs across various sectors (World Bank, 2023). An anticipated shortage of 85.3 million skilled workers by 2030 could cost the global economy $8.5 trillion, while climate change risks may trim 1.5% off global GDP by 2060 (Korn Ferry, 2023; King's College London, 2024). Firms that successfully integrate RGM strategies have been shown to retain 15% more revenue during economic crises (McKinsey, 2023).

Previously, I unveiled ineffective methodologies through Profit Play 1, ignited revenue streams with Profit Play 2, optimised promotional strategies in Profit Play 3, balanced portfolios with Profit Play 4, slashed costs through Profit Play 5, enhanced go-to-market approaches in Profit Play 6, trimmed overheads in Profit Play 7, uplifted workforce capabilities in Profit Play 8, mastered out-of-stock challenges in Profit Play 9, and championed ESG initiatives in Profit Play 10. Profit Play 11 masterfully amalgamates these efforts into a harmonious symphony while setting the stage for a legacy-building Profit Play 12 (if applicable).

The Problem: Why You're Leaving Profits on the Table

Siloed profit levers—pricing, promotions, procurement, overhead, workforce, supply chain, and ESG—give rise to dissonance that drains Free Cash Flow (FCF), Return on Equity (ROE), and Sustainable Growth Rate (SGR) in both Indian and Middle Eastern markets.

Isolated Pricing and Promotions: The Revenue Leak

Dysfunctional pricing and promotions, and a lack of support from the supply chain or ESG initiatives, result in stockouts and eroded consumer trust. In 2023, a Kolkata FMCG SME faced severe challenges with incorrectly priced biscuits, which, combined with a 15% OOS rate, annihilated ₹80 crore in potential revenue. By implementing dynamic pricing and forging strong supply chain connections, we managed to recuperate ₹50 crore, thereby aligning with a 9% SGR (IBEF, 2023). A Dubai SME, lacking the backing for its promotional strategies, suffered a setback of AED 5 million (Gulf News, August

2023*). A price elasticity of less than 1.5 risks losing 5–10% in revenue (McKinsey, 2023).

Submetrics that you should Target

- ✓ **Sub-Metric: Price Elasticity**
- ✓ **Target:** >1.5 for revenue optimisation
- ✓ **Regional Nuance:** Dynamic pricing is essential for India's kiranas, while the Middle East's luxury markets require focused promotions
- ✓ **Mini-Framework:** Conduct an AI audit on pricing, synchronise with the supply chain; utilise Power BI to monitor elasticity

Fragmented Operations: The Efficiency Gap

Disconnected procurement, supply chain mechanisms, and overhead structures engender waste. A Chennai SME suffered from overstocked inventory, which wasted ₹30 crore due to a damaging 12% OOS rate. Implementing AI-driven procurement strategies yielded a significant ₹20 crore in savings while achieving a 10% SGR (NASSCOM, 2023). Similarly, a Qatar SME's fragmented logistics resulted in losses of QAR 200,000 (Gulf News, August 2023*). OOS rates exceeding 2% typically contribute to a loss of 4–8% in sales (IBEF, 2023).

Submetrics that you should Target

- ✓ **Sub-Metric:** Out-of-Stock (OOS) Rate
- ✓ **Target: Issue:** Chennai SME's 12% OOS caused them ₹30 crore in losses.

- ✓ **Regional Nuance:** Indian SMEs need AI-based forecasting, while the Middle East requires enhanced blockchain transparency.
- ✓ **Mini-Framework:** Perform a supply chain audit (1 month), deploy IoT solutions, and use Shiprocket for ongoing OOS monitoring.

Weak ESG Integration: The Risk Trap

Fragile ESG practices can incur hefty fines and alienate potential investors. In 2023, a Surat SME saw fines of ₹10 crore due to non-compliance with ESG regulations (IBEF, 2023). Moreover, a Saudi SME overlooked AED 3 million in green fund opportunities (Gulf News, August 2023*). ESG scores below 80 diminish investment attractiveness by 20% (PwC Middle East, 2023).

- ✓ **Submetrics that you should Target**
- ✓ **Sub-Metric:** ESG Score
- ✓ **Target:** >80 for improved investor appeal
- ✓ **Regional Nuance:** India's firms must comply with BRSR, while the Middle East firms align with Vision 2030.
- ✓ **Mini-Framework:** Conduct an ESG audit (1 month); implement renewable energy solutions; integrate AI for ongoing monitoring.

In 2021, a Mumbai SME learned the hard way when mispriced snacks and a 10% OOS rate resulted in an astounding ₹50 crore loss. Through the integration of RGM across pricing, procurement, and ESG, we salvaged an additional ₹300 crore, not unlike a vendor mastering the art of biryani preparation.

In 2022, a Riyadh SME penalised by supply chain delays lost AED 50 million; the implementation of AI in forecasting and ESG adjustments redeemed a notable ₹250 crore. In 2023, a Bangalore SME suffered a loss of ₹1 crore due to disconnected profit levers. Still, RGM alignment enabled us to recover the entire profit amount, akin to a chai stall perfectly synchronising the serving of cups alongside pricing. These experiences have led to the development of the SEE, SHAPE, SCALE, SUSTAIN, OPTIMIZE, MONITOR framework.

The Solution: Your Profit Playbook

The SEE, SHAPE, SCALE, SUSTAIN, OPTIMIZE, MONITOR framework is designed to orchestrate all profit levers within a coherent RGM strategy, guaranteeing "zero waste, max profit."

Step 1: SEE – Audit Levers with Analytics

Map out pricing, promotions, procurement, overhead, workforce, supply chains, and ESG through a Profit Impact Index (PII) (on a 1–5 scale).

- ✓ **Metric:** PII (>4 for meaningful impact).
- ✓ **Regional Tip:** Focus on pricing audits in India; ESG integration is key in the Middle East.
- ✓ **Mini-Checklist:** Conduct a lever audit (1 month); chart out PII; pinpoint discrepancies.

Step 2: SHAPE – Optimise Pricing & Promotions

Align dynamic pricing strategies and targeted promotions with supply chain and ESG efforts.

- ✓ **Metric:** Price Elasticity (>1.5).
- ✓ **Regional Tip:** India's kiranas require dynamic pricing; the Middle East markets benefit from well-targeted promotions.
- ✓ **Mini-Checklist:** Analyse demand (1 month); set dynamic pricing protocols; monitor elasticity.

Step 3: SCALE – Streamline Procurement & Supply Chain

Integrate streamlined procurement processes and synchronised supply chains with workforce and ESG considerations.

- ✓ **Metric:** OOS Rate.
- ✓ **Regional Tip:** India benefits from AI forecasting; the Middle East should implement blockchain efficiencies.
- ✓ **Mini-Checklist:** Execute a procurement audit (1 month); implement IoT solutions; continuously monitor OOS.

Step 4: SUSTAIN – Enhance Workforce Capabilities

Empower teams through AI-driven tools focused on pricing, supply chain efficiencies, and ESG alignment.

- ✓ **Metric:** Skill Level Index (>4).
- ✓ **Regional Tip:** India should prioritise ethical selling practices; the Middle East needs enhanced ESG training.
- ✓ **Mini-Checklist:** Evaluate current skill levels (1 month); provide AI training; track progress through indices.

Step 5: OPTIMIZE – Lean Overhead & ESG

Reduce manufacturing overhead (MOH) and operating expenses (OPEX) while integrating ESG through AI and IoT innovations.

- ✓ **Regional Tip:** Compliance with BRSR is essential in India; alignment with Vision 2030 is critical in the Middle East.
- ✓ **Mini-Checklist:** Audit operational costs (1 month); deploy IoT technologies; continuously evaluate ESG scores.

Step 6: MONITOR – Track with RGM Dashboard

Utilise an AI-driven dashboard to ensure all levers are in sync.

- ✓ **Metric:** RGM Revenue Growth (>10% annually).
- ✓ **Regional Tip:** India should focus on pricing oversight; the Middle East needs robust ESG monitoring.

✓ **Mini-Checklist:** Develop a comprehensive dashboard (1 month); track KPIs; adapt strategies as necessary.

Future Outlook

By 2030, the integration of AI, blockchain, and IoT technology will significantly amplify RGM capabilities, propelling SME profit margins by 20% within India's $160 billion e-commerce space and in the digital retail sector of the Middle East (Times of India, January 2025; Gulf News, August 2023*). Anticipated AI-driven pricing enhancements could reduce losses by 30%, while implementing blockchain governance may unlock an estimated 40% increase in green funding opportunities. Furthermore, ESG mandates stand to drive revenue growth by 15%, ensuring the bold promise of zero waste and maximum profit (McKinsey, 2023; FICCI, 2024).

Disclaimer for Profit Surge: Business Strategies for Epic Profit Growth.

The examples, case studies, and financial figures presented in this book are derived from publicly available data, industry reports, and reasonable estimates based on standard business practices and market trends. They only illustrate strategic concepts and operational insights for educational and informational purposes. The author and publisher have made every effort to ensure the accuracy of the information at the time of publication. Still, specific financial outcomes, losses, or gains attributed to companies are estimates and should not be construed as precise historical records or proprietary information.

No confidential or proprietary data has been used, and the examples are not intended to imply any endorsement, criticism, or verification by the companies mentioned. Readers are encouraged to research and consult professional advisors before applying the strategies discussed. The author and publisher disclaim any liability for actions taken based on the information provided.

The appendix includes a detailed bibliography and links to publicly accessible sources such as company annual reports, news articles, and industry analyses to provide transparency and facilitate further exploration of the referenced data.

The Coda of Prosperity: Sustaining the Profit Symphony

As we conclude our Profit Symphony, we reflect on the vital work we have accomplished together in creating strategies for lasting prosperity. Throughout the eleven sections of this playbook, we have addressed the vibrant markets of India and the Middle East, turning challenges into opportunities with careful consideration. Each Profit Play—from identifying hidden leaks to driving revenue, optimising trade spend, balancing portfolios, reducing COGS, connecting products to customers, streamlining overhead, enhancing workforce potential, overcoming supply chain disruptions, embedding sustainability, and pursuing zero-waste profitability—has contributed valuable insights and practical advice.

This effort started with a vision to move beyond the Profit Mirage, where top-line success can sometimes disguise eroded margins. Our goal has been to shape a future where every decision adds value, much like a guiding star for those navigating unfamiliar waters. We have worked through complex markets and used technology to support our aims. The SEE, SHAPE, SCALE framework has been our guide, helping businesses evaluate their challenges and develop clear solutions.

I want to take a moment to express my gratitude for your patience throughout this process. I hope I have helped craft your strategies. The markets of India and the Middle East require resilience and careful planning. As e-commerce grows and sustainability becomes increasingly important, your business needs to remain adaptable, adjusting to changes like a ship adjusting its sails to the shifting winds. You can maintain profitability by embracing tools like AI, IoT, and blockchain, focusing on ESG principles, and fostering a culture of continuous improvement.

As you move ahead, let this playbook guide you toward substantial growth while minimising waste. The tools—Power BI, SAP Ariba, Zoho, and MCX APIs—and strategies we discussed are designed to help you find success. Whether a micro, small, or medium enterprise (MSME) or a multinational corporation, your organisation is well-positioned to lead, like a lighthouse providing direction in a storm.

Thank you for your collaboration. I hope you can sustain this symphony and see your efforts reflected in the profits that resonate across markets, creating a legacy of strategic clarity.